Casserole

COOKBOOK

Natalie Wilkins

TABLE OF CONTENTS

INTRODUCTION

Casseroles may remind you of a combination of 19th-century convenience foods baked in the oven. However, since the development of ceramic cooking utensils, casseroles have retained their historical significance. Casseroles have evolved to integrate regional food tastes. They may be an elegant and healthy addition to any dinner, despite their humble origins and frequent use to stretch expensive ingredients to serve many. Making casseroles with a variety of good grains, lean meats, vegetarian meat substitutes, fresh veggies, and herbs is simple. Use processed foods carefully, such as canned beans, packaged broths, or tinned chopped tomatoes. Most casseroles are linked together by a sauce or gravy; therefore, fatty components are not necessary to keep them wet. Typically, all that is required before assembly is a small mist of nonstick spray.

Even while casseroles are frequently served as main dishes, practically anything, including appetizers and desserts, can be transformed into a casserole—often with wonderful results. The richness of summer food, such as maize and tomatoes, or the juiciness of ripe berries, is best displayed when baked into a meal. The term "cereal casserole" can describe both the prepared dish and the baking dish in which it is baked. You can prepare dinner in a single pot and cut down on cleanup time by using most casserole dishes on the stovetop and in the oven. The meal is typically prepared with meat, such as beef or pig, but it can also be prepared using chicken or fish. In addition to a starchy binder like pasta or rice and a cheese topping on the side, it is frequently served with chopped veggies. Additionally, liquids are used in the cooking of meals. These foods include, among others, broth, wine, vegetable juice, creamy soup, and cider.

Making casseroles in casserole pans can be done in a variety of ways. Here are a few examples of how casseroles can be prepared:

- For a meatless supper, vegetarian casserole recipes include vegetables. Typically, a cheese or breadcrumb topping is added to vegetable casseroles.
- A variety of sauces, including cheese sauce, tomato sauce, and cream sauce, may also be the foundation of a casserole.
- Fish, meat, or vegetables can all be used to make these casseroles.
- A milk-based sauce may also serve as the foundation for a casserole.

This cookbook has more than 120+ recipes that can be fried, baked, broiled, steamed, braised, and then broiled again, which is fantastic. Are you anticipating making these recipes? Bring your creativity to the kitchen by drawing inspiration from these dishes. Enjoy!

CHAPTER 1:
TIPS AND TRICKS

Even though making a casserole requires some initial work, after it is put together, it may be baked whenever you want. Even greater, after resting in the refrigerator, the flavors usually mellow and become even more delicious.

Prep Casseroles Ahead

The majority of casseroles can be prepared in advance without much of the recipe changing. When it's time to bake it, simply cover the prepared casserole with plastic wrap or a lid and store it in the refrigerator.

It's usually a good idea to make and add biscuits, crumbles, or cobbler toppings to recipes right before a bake so they don't get mushy. When making fresh bread crumbs, you might be able to make the topper as you make the casserole. Add it just before the dish goes into the oven, after setting it aside.

The added time to bake a chilled casserole from the refrigerator could be up to 20 minutes. Take the casserole's temperature to make sure it is fully cooked. It should be baked until the center measures a temperature of 165°F or above. The dish needs longer baking time if the temperature is below 165°F.

Freeze Casseroles

The best casseroles to freeze are those with a lot of moisture, as freezing tends to dry foods. Stews, simmered foods, and saucy lasagnas keep in the freezer exceptionally well. Additionally, baked casseroles typically freeze poorly compared to unbaked casseroles. To make it easier to defrost a casserole you intend to eat in one sitting, it's a good idea to split it into a single serving before freezing.

It is possible to freeze a casserole in the pan it will be cooked in, but doing so uses up the freezer area (additionally, you can't use your pan while the casserole is frozen.) Alternately, before constructing and freezing your casserole dish, top it with nonstick foil or foil that has been treated with nonstick spray.

Defrost frozen casseroles overnight in the fridge (not on the table) before baking according to the recipe's instructions.

Reheat Casseroles

Heat up only the amount of the dish you'll be eating all at once. This will stop the remaining casserole from dehydrating and aid in preventing the formation of germs on the dish's unfinished section.

To reheat casseroles, use a microwave's reheat setting or an oven tuned to a reduced temperature than the casserole was cooked at first. To ensure that the food heats consistently, ensure to let the casserole rest after microwaving it for a minute or two.

Healthy Cooking Guidelines

According to the majority of nutrition and health specialists, a balanced diet should include a range of fruits and vegetables, whole grains, lean meats and poultry, seafood, low-fat or fat-free milk, eggs, legumes and peas, and nuts and seeds. Additionally, it limits the daily intake of salt, fatty foods, added sugars, and processed carbs.

Your body cannot digest the type of carbohydrate known as fiber. Fiber-rich diets have been demonstrated to support intestinal health, lower blood cholesterol, promote weight loss, and regulate blood sugar levels. Vegetables, fruits, entire grains, and legumes all contain fiber.

Of course, within this foundation of healthy eating, there are innumerable ways to tailor eating regimens to make them vegetarian, vegan, dairy- and wheat-free, or just to your preferences. When you cook your own dishes, it's easier to keep track of what you consume, and with some practice, you can make several meals that are actually satisfying, delicious, and healthy.

Carbohydrates

Given the recent controversy surrounding carbohydrates, you might believe that the best strategy for preserving a healthy weight is to avoid them completely. In actuality, carbohydrates serve as the body's main fuel source. For your muscles, intestines, kidneys, brain, and central nervous system to work effectively, you must include them in your diet. They need to account for between 45% and 65% of the calories in our diet, according to the United States Department of Agriculture.

Food experts separate simple and complicated carbs into two groups. Simple carbohydrates include sugar molecules, including fructose, dextrose, glucose, and sucrose. Chains of three or more linked sugar units constitute complex carbohydrates. Remember to stick with largely whole food sources of carbohydrates rather than getting caught up in these labels, which don't describe how your body utilizes either molecule. Legumes, fruits, vegetables, and whole grains are examples of whole-food carbohydrates (grains that have the endosperm, germ, and bran). They supply you with a wonderful dose of nutrients and minerals. They also energize you. Contrarily, during the refining process, essential vitamins and minerals are removed from refined products like white rice, white flour, and simple sugars.

Protein

When your body doesn't have enough carbohydrates, you use the protein in your diet to manufacture hormones and enzymes, build and repair tissue, maintain a strong immune system, and use it as an energy source. The USDA recommends that between 10% and 35% of calories come from protein. Nine amino acids make up a protein, and because the body is incapable of creating them, they are considered "vital." All nine of the required amino acids are present in the animal proteins found in meat, fish, eggs, and milk, making them "whole" proteins.
Except for soy, plant proteins are thought to be incomplete and must be consumed in combination to supply all nine essential amino acids. A good illustration of this would be serving rice and beans together. Protein can be found in whole grains, beans, nuts, seeds, and other veggies.

Fats

The USDA advises that between 20% and 35% of your daily calories originate from fat. This quantity is necessary for healthy organ functioning, energy, normal growth and development, and the absorption of fat-soluble vitamins (A, E, D, and K).
Although it may be present in certain tropical oils, saturated fat is mostly derived from animal-based diets. It is stable at room temperature and shouldn't account for more than 7% of your daily calorie consumption. Saturated fat consumption can cause blood cholesterol to increase.
When liquid vegetable oils are hydrogenated to solidify them for usage in commercial products like stick margarine and shortenings, trans fats are created. These lipids elevate LDL ("bad") levels in the blood. Trans fat should make up less than 1% of a person's daily recommended calorie consumption, according to the American Heart Association. One of the healthiest forms of fat is mono- and polyunsaturated. They are derived from plant-based sources such as avocados, nuts, seeds, and plant oils (such as safflower, olive, and corn). There is proof that using these oils in the diet with saturated fats may help lower blood cholesterol levels.

Cholesterol

A waxy molecule called cholesterol is found in all areas of your body. Numerous hormones, bile acids that aid in fat digestion, and vitamin D are all produced using it. The liver makes cholesterol, although it can also be obtained from the diet. It is contained in foods made from animals and is referred to as dietary cholesterol. A condition known as atherosclerosis, or the buildup of fat and cholesterol in artery walls, is brought on by having too much cholesterol in circulation. The 2010 Dietary Guidelines for Americans suggests that dietary cholesterol intake should be under 300 mg daily.

<u>**Minerals and Vitamins**</u>

If you consume a variety of foods while meeting your calorie demands, your body will normally acquire the majority of the vitamins and minerals it requires for maximum health. Some individuals, such as vegans who avoid animal protein or pregnant or nursing moms, may require supplemental dietary supplements of certain essential nutrients. With the help of your registered dietitian and doctor, you can decide whether you ought to start taking supplements or alter your current diet.

<u>**Sodium**</u>

A relatively minimal amount of sodium, an essential nutrient, is required for normal bodily function unless there are significant sweating losses. It is well established that consuming more sodium raises blood pressure, whereas consuming less sodium in the diet lowers blood pressure.

For most adults, the 2010 Dietary Guidelines for Americans advise limiting sodium intake to under 2,300 mg per day; for African Americans, people with high blood pressure, diabetes, or chronic renal disease, as well as people over fifty-one, the best suggestion is less than 1,500 mg per day.

<u>**Sugars**</u>

Sugars are naturally found in foods, including fruits, vegetables, and dairy products; nevertheless, most people need to restrict the added sugars they consume to keep their daily calorie requirements. Sodas, sweets, and several snack foods, sauces, and condiments, are examples of foods containing added sugars. Carefully read the labels before deciding.

Tips for Cooking Rice

Boil the water before adding rice. This is a must! Cooking rice in a saucepan covered with a lid is crucial. Rice will uniformly cook by absorbing the water. You can cook rice without a lid on the pan, but you'll need to use more water, which can take longer. When cooked in this manner, the rice could also be mushier.

- When cooking rice, add a few drops of Tabasco sauce to the boiling water to enhance the rice's flavor.
- When cooking rice, 2 tablespoons of vinegar added to the boiling water enhances the flavor of the rice. Instead of vinegar, you can also substitute fresh lemon juice.
- Prepare the rice in chicken broth rather than water to give it more taste. For added flavor, try cooking the rice with wine, beer, or fruit juices. Wine, beer, or fruit juices can be used in place of up to half of the water required to cook the rice.
- After the rice reaches a boil, do not disturb it. It will gum up the rice.

Cooked rice stored in the refrigerator may be eaten even after a few days have passed, although five is the limit. For three months, cooked rice can be frozen. Rice may be easily used in recipes after being frozen. I freeze portions of rice that are one cup. If using the rice in a casserole or main dish, there is no need to thaw it first. For each cup of leftover rice you want to reheat, add 2 teaspoons of water. Rice can be heated in a saucepan or a microwave. Rice should simmer in a pan over low heat until it is hot and fluffy.

CHAPTER 2:
BREAKFAST RECIPES

1. Bacon, Egg, and Spinach Breakfast Casserole

Preparation Time: 15 minutes

Cooking Time: 20 minutes

Servings: 5

Ingredients:

- 1 ½ c. Egg whites (approx. 12 eggs worth)
- 2 large eggs, fresh, whole, raw
- 2 c. Spinach, frozen
- 4 strips of bacon
- 1 c. pieces or slices of Mushrooms, fresh
- ½ c. chopped Green Peppers (bell peppers)
- ½ c. chopped Peppers, sweet, red, fresh
- 2 c. Shredded Sharp Cheddar Cheese
- ½ of a medium (2-½ " dia) Onion, raw

Directions:

1. Spray cooking oil in a 9x13 pan. Utilize a smaller casserole dish if you prefer a thicker portion.
2. Dry off, drain, and thaw the spinach. As much moisture as you can remove from it. Additionally, I used sautéed fresh spinach.
3. Preheat oven to 375°F. Set the heat to medium-high and place the vegetables in the skillet (excluding the spinach). Until vegetables are tender, saute.
4. Vegetables should cover the entire bottom of the baking dish.
5. Include the cooked spinach. Salt and pepper the egg whites and eggs after whisking them together. Over the vegetables, evenly distribute the egg mixture.
6. Add bacon strip crumbles. Add some cheddar cheese, shredded
7. For 35 minutes, bake. Before eating, remove from oven and let cool.

Nutritional Information:

Calories: 459

Total fat: 30 g

Carbs: 52 g

Fiber: 19 g

Protein: 8 g

2. Berry Cream Cheese French Toast Casserole

Preparation Time: 15 minutes

Cooking Time: 30 minutes

Servings: 4

Ingredients:

- 4-6 slices of day-old French bread, cubed
- 4 eggs
- ¼ c. brown sugar
- 1 tsp. vanilla extract
- ½ tsp. cinnamon
- A pinch of allspice
- 1 ½ c. milk
- ½ c. blueberries
- ½ c. strawberries, sliced
- 2 oz. cream cheese, diced
- Cooking spray
- Optional toppings: maple syrup, whipped cream, icing sugar

Directions:

1. Preheat the oven to 350°F. An 8x8" baking dish's bottom should be lightly greased. The bread cubes should be put in a big bowl.
2. In a medium bowl, combine the milk, eggs, brown sugar, vanilla, cinnamon, and allspice. After spreading the custard mixture over the bread, let it sit for 10 minutes while occasionally stirring.
3. Pour half the bread mixture into the bottom of the pan. Sprinkle half the berries and cream cheese on top. Top with remaining bread mixture, berries, and cheese.
4. Bake, covered, for 20 minutes. Uncover and bake for 10 more minutes or until the bread is golden brown and the casserole is set. Serve alone or with desired toppings.

Nutritional Information:

Calories: 335

Fat: 10 g

Carbs: 50 g

Protein: 13 g

Sodium: 453 mg

3. Gobble Gobble Spinach and Mushroom Egg Bake

Preparation Time: 15 minutes

Cooking Time: 40 minutes

Servings: 4

Ingredients:

- 1 tbsp. olive oil
- 1 lb. turkey sausage
- 1 medium onion, diced
- 1 clove of garlic, minced
- 8 oz. frozen or fresh spinach
- 1 c. mushrooms, sliced
- ¼ c. carrot, grated
- 2 tbsps. fresh basil, chopped
- Salt and pepper to taste
- 6 eggs
- ½ c. milk
- 3 oz. feta, crumbled

Directions:

1. Set the oven to 400°F and spray a 9x13" casserole dish with cooking spray.
2. Warm up a tablespoon of olive oil in a skillet and cook the sausage and onion for about 10 minutes, until the sausage is lightly browned and the onion is translucent.
3. Stir in the garlic, spinach, mushrooms, carrot, basil, salt, and pepper. Place the sausage and vegetables in the prepared casserole dish.
4. Whisk the eggs and milk in a mixing bowl, and pour it over the sausage and veggie mixture. Top with feta. Bake for 20 minutes, until the cheese, is melted and the eggs are set.

Nutritional Information:

Calories: 187

Fat: 11 g

Carbs: 4 g

Protein: 17 g

Sodium: 699 mg

4. Jalapeno Popper Casseroles

Preparation Time: 15 minutes

Cooking Time: 30 minutes

Servings: 3

Ingredients:

- 24 oz. Chicken Breast (cooked), no skin, roasted
- 2 slices of thick-cut bacon
- 1 oz. Sharp Cheddar Cheese
- 12 oz. Cream Cheese
- 12 tsps. hot sauce - Cholula hot sauce
- 4 Jalapeno Peppers

Directions:

1. For 20 minutes, bake chicken at 400°F. Sliced jalapenos and bacon should be softened in a skillet.
2. Stir until creamy after adding the spicy sauce and cream cheese.
3. To prepare the chicken for baking, chop or shred it. Lay mixture over the chicken, then sprinkle cheese on top.
4. Bake for 10-15 minutes at 400°F, then broil until cheese is browned.

Nutritional Information:

Calories: 343

Total fat: 14 g

Carbs: 55 g

Fiber: 8 g

Protein: 6 g

5. Mexican Casserole

Preparation Time: 15 minutes

Cooking Time: 30 minutes

Servings: 4

Ingredients:

- 2 c. Mexican cheese blend
- 4 oz. cream cheese
- 3 eggs
- ⅓ c. cream
- ¼ c. parmesan cheese
- 1 small can of diced green chilies
- 1 tsp. chili powder
- 1 lb. ground beef and chopped onion to taste, browned in 4 tsps. taco seasoning

Directions:

1. Preheat oven to 350°F. Beat together cream cheese and eggs until smooth. Stir in cream, parmesan cheese, green chilies, and spices.
2. Spray 9 x 13 pan with nonstick oil. Sprinkle 2 cups of Mexican cheese blend into the dish. Spread ground beef over the cheese mixture and pour the egg mixture over it. Bake for 35 minutes. Let stand for 5 minutes.
3. It can be served with sliced tomato, salsa, and sour cream.

Nutrional Information:

Calories: 343

Total fat: 14 g

Carbs: 55 g

Fiber: 8 g

Protein: 6 g

6. Mushroom Hash Brown Morning Casserole

Preparation Time: 15 minutes
Cooking Time: 45 minutes
Servings: 6

Ingredients:

- 2 medium potatoes
- 8 slices of pork bacon
- 1 ½ c. onion, chopped
- 8 oz. shiitake mushrooms, sliced
- 2 cloves garlic, minced
- ¼ c. chicken stock
- 5 c. fresh baby spinach
- 2 tbsps. fresh parsley, chopped
- Salt and pepper to taste
- ½ c. cheddar cheese, shredded, divided
- ½ c. milk
- 6 large eggs, lightly beaten
- Cooking spray

Directions:

1. Preheat the oven to 350°F and spray an 11x17" broiler-safe pan with cooking spray.
2. Peel and shred the potatoes. Line a colander with a clean kitchen towel and place the potatoes inside. Rinse well, gather the towel, and squeeze out as much liquid from the potatoes as possible. Set aside in the towel.
3. Cook the bacon in a large, non-stick skillet over medium-high heat until crisp. Remove the bacon from the pan, chop it, and set it aside to cool.
4. Drain all but one tablespoon of grease from the pan. Add the onion, mushrooms, and garlic, and sauté for 5 minutes, until they are softened and slightly browned.
5. Add the shredded potatoes and chicken stock. Cook for 5 minutes, stirring frequently.
6. Add the spinach and parsley, and season with salt and pepper. Cook briefly until the spinach wilts.
7. Remove the skillet from the heat. Stir in the crumbled bacon and half the cheese.
8. Place the mushroom mixture in the prepared baking dish. (If you like, you can place it in the fridge at this point and continue with the next steps in the morning.)
9. Combine the milk and eggs and pour them over the vegetable mixture. Bake at 350°F for 25 minutes.
10. In the final minutes of baking, sprinkle the remaining cheese on top of the casserole. Turn on the broiler and cook until melted.

Nutritional Information: Calories: 278, Fat: 10 g, Carbs: 21 g, Protein: 17 g, Sodium: 618 mg

7. Quinoa Breakfast Casserole

Preparation Time: 15 minutes

Cooking Time: 60 minutes

Servings: 4

Ingredients:

- 1 ½ c. warm water
- ¼ c. brewed coffee, hot or warm
- 2 tbsps. fresh or canned pumpkin purée
- 1 tbsp. maple syrup
- 1 tsp. Coconut oil, melted
- ¼ tsp. pure vanilla extract
- 1 tsp. pumpkin pie spice
- ½ c. dry quinoa

For the Topping:

- ¼ c. chopped nuts
- 2 tbsps. oat flour
- 2 tbsps. honey
- 1 tbsp. Almond flour
- ½ tsp. cinnamon
- A pinch of salt
- 1 tbsp. coconut oil

Directions:

1. Preheat the oven to 350°F.
2. Combine the water, coffee, pumpkin purée, maple syrup, coconut oil, vanilla, and pumpkin pie spice in a small casserole dish. Stir to combine.
3. Add the quinoa, and stir.
4. Cover and bake for 45–50 minutes until most of the liquid is gone.
5. Meanwhile, combine the nuts, oat flour, honey, almond flour, cinnamon, and salt in a small bowl. Stir in the coconut oil, and set aside.
6. Once the casserole is done, remove it from the oven, and sprinkle it with the topping. Return it to the oven, uncovered, and bake for another 10 minutes until the topping browns.

Nutritional Information: Calories: 197, Fat: 12 g, Carbs: 20 g, Protein: 3 g, Sodium: 43 mg

8. Reuben Casserole

Preparation Time: 15 minutes

Cooking Time: 30 minutes

Servings: 4

Ingredients:

- 3 lb. Steamed Cauliflower
- 3 lb. corned beef shredded into ½" pieces
- 2 lb. Sauerkraut
- 1 lb. swiss cheese (shredded or slices)
- 1 pt. Heavy Whipping Cream
- 4 tbsps. Non-Salted Butter
- 2 tbsps. Ground Mustard Powder
- Caraway Seed (if desired)

Directions:

1. Heat oven to 350 °F. Spray 9x14 inch glass baking dish with cooking spray.
2. Steam cauliflower, then adds butter. Once butter is melted, add heavy whipping cream and mash-up
3. Spread ½ of the cauliflower in a baking dish. Top with ½ the corned beef. Spread ½ the sauerkraut over corned beef. Spoon the remaining cauliflower over the top; spread gently.
4. Spread the remaining corned beef, the remaining sauerkraut, and the remaining swiss cheese. Add caraway seed if desired.
5. Bake uncovered for 25-30 minutes.

Nutritional Information:

Calories: 244

Total fat: 6 g

Carbs: 30 g

Fiber: 6 g

Protein: 7 g

9. Roasted Broccoli and Ham Breakfast Casserole

Preparation Time: 15 minutes

Cooking Time: 30 minutes

Servings: 4

Ingredients:

- 1 head of broccoli, florets only, cut into bite-sized pieces
- 2 tbsps. olive oil
- Salt and pepper, to taste
- 1 c. cooked ham, cubed
- ½ c. Parmesan or Romana cheese, grated
- 1 red bell pepper, finely chopped
- 3 scallions, chopped
- 12 eggs
- 2 tsps. herbes de Provence

Directions:

1. Preheat the oven to 425°F and prepare a 9x13" casserole dish with cooking spray.
2. In a large bowl, combine the broccoli with the olive oil, salt, and pepper; transfer to a baking sheet.
3. Roast for 25 minutes until browned, and remove the pan from the oven. Reduce the oven temperature to 375°F.
4. Gently combine the roasted broccoli, ham, Parmesan, red bell pepper, and scallions in a large bowl. Move the mixture to the prepared baking dish.
5. In a large mixing bowl, lightly beat the eggs, and stir in the herbes de Provence. With salt and pepper, season it. Pour over the broccoli mixture.
6. Bake for 35 minutes, until the surface is lightly browned and the eggs are cooked.

Nutritional Information:

Calories: 249

Fat: 17 g

Carbs: 3 g

Protein: 16 g

Sodium: 361 mg

10. Sausage and Spiced Apple Breakfast Casserole

Preparation Time: 15 minutes

Cooking Time: 55 minutes

Servings: 4

Ingredients:

- 6 large, pre-cooked maple-flavored pork breakfast sausages
- 10 eggs
- 3 c. milk
- 1 tsp. vanilla
- 1 tsp. salt
- 2 large apples, peeled and chopped
- 2 tbsps. brown sugar
- 1 tsp. ground cinnamon
- 8 c. whole wheat bread, cubed
- 2 c. shredded cheddar cheese, divided

Directions:

1. Slice the sausages into rounds and set them aside.
2. Whisk together the eggs, milk, vanilla, and salt in a large bowl until well blended.
3. Mix the apples, sugar, and cinnamon in a separate bowl until well coated.
4. Grease a 9x13" baking dish, and place half the bread cubes in the bottom. Top with half the sausage, half the apple mixture, and half the cheese. Repeat the layers.
5. Pour the egg mixture over the casserole, and coat it all with the egg mixture evenly.
6. Refrigerate overnight to allow the bread to soak up a lot of the egg mixture.
7. When morning comes, remove the casserole from the fridge and preheat the oven to 325°F.
8. Bake the casserole for 55–60 minutes, or until a knife inserted in the center comes out clean.

Nutritional Information:

Calories: 314

Fat: 18 g

Carbs: 23 g

Protein: 16 g

Sodium: 161 mg

11. Sweet and Savory Breakfast Casserole

Preparation Time: 15 minutes

Cooking Time: 40 minutes

Servings: 4

Ingredients:

- 1 tsp. olive oil
- 12 oz. turkey breakfast sausage
- 2 c. milk
- 2 c. egg substitute
- 1 tsp. dry mustard
- Salt and pepper to taste
- A pinch of red pepper flakes
- 3 large eggs
- 1 loaf of white bread
- 1 c. cheddar cheese, shredded
- Cooking spray
- ¼ c. green onion, chopped
- Paprika, for sprinkling

Directions:

1. Heat a large, non-stick skillet over medium-high heat, and heat the olive oil. To the pan, add the sausage and cook for 5 minutes or until browned, stirring and crumbling the sausage.
2. Take it away from the heat and let it cool. Combine the milk, egg substitute, mustard, salt, pepper, red pepper flakes, and eggs in a large bowl, and whisk thoroughly. Trim the crusts from the bread and cut them into 1-inch cubes.
3. Add the bread cubes, sausage, and cheddar cheese to the custard mixture, stirring to combine. Pour it into a 9x13" baking dish or a 3-quart casserole dish coated with cooking spray, spreading it evenly. Cover the dish and put it in the fridge for 8 hours or overnight.
4. In the morning (or when you're ready to cook), preheat the oven to 350°F. Take the casserole from the refrigerator and let it stand for 30 minutes. Sprinkle with green onion and paprika.
5. For 45 minutes or until set and lightly browned, bake the casserole at 350°F. Let stand for 10 minutes.

Nutritional Information: Calories: 245, Fat: 2 g, Carbs: 20 g, Protein: 9 g, Sodium: 609 mg

12. Pumpkin French Toast

Preparation Time: 15 minutes

Cooking Time: 35 minutes

Servings: 4

Ingredients:

- 6–7 c. 1-inch bread cubes
- 7 large eggs
- 2 c. milk
- 1 tsp. vanilla extract
- 2 tsps. pumpkin pie spice
- ½ c. pumpkin purée
- Cooking spray
- 4 tbsps. Maple syrup for topping
- Optional: additional spice, nuts, raisins, shredded coconut, chopped apricots or dates

Directions:

1. The night before, spray a 9x13" baking dish with cooking spray and fill it with bread cubes.
2. Whisk the eggs, milk, vanilla, pumpkin purée, and pie spice until well combined in a large bowl. Pour it over the bread and gently push it down with a spoon until the bread is moistened or immersed. Cover, and refrigerate overnight.
3. In the morning, preheat the oven to 350°F.
4. Uncover the casserole and top with brown sugar, additional pumpkin pie spice, fruit, and nuts (optional).
5. For 35–45 minutes or until golden brown, bake and set.
6. Drizzle with maple syrup and serve.

Nutritional Information:

Calories: 122

Fat: 4 g

Carbs: 14 g

Protein: 8 g

Sodium: 145 mg

13. Ground Turkey Casserole

Preparation Time: 15 minutes

Cooking Time: 60 minutes

Servings: 4

Ingredients:

- 1 lb. ground turkey
- 1 (15 oz.) can of tomato sauce
- 1 tsp. white sugar
- 1 (8 oz.) container of sour cream
- 1 (8 oz.) package of cream cheese
- 1 (12 oz.) package of uncooked egg noodles
- 2 c. shredded Cheddar cheese

Directions:

1. Set the oven to a heat of 175°C or 350°F to preheat.
2. Sauté ground turkey in a big skillet on medium-high heat until browned, about 5-10 minutes. Drain the turkey, stir in sugar and tomato sauce and put aside. Mix cream cheese and sour cream in a medium bowl, then blend well and put aside.
3. Following package directions to cook noodles. Transfer noodles into a 13"x9" baking dish, then layer noodles with the turkey mixture. Layer the turkey mixture with the sour cream mixture and put cheese on top.
4. Bake for 20-35 minutes at 175°C or 350°F, until the cheese has melted and bubbles.

Nutritional Information:

Calories: 287

Total fat: 12 g

Carbs: 41 g

Fiber: 6 g

Protein: 8 g

14. Gumbo Casserole

Preparation Time: 15 minutes

Cooking Time: 50 minutes

Servings: 4

Ingredients:

- 1 c. frozen okra, thawed
- 1 tsp. Dried minced onion
- ½ tsp. Cajun seasoning
- ½ lb. cooked ham, diced
- ½ tsp. garlic powder
- 1 (10.75 oz.) can water
- ½ lb. of shrimp, cooked, peeled, and deveined
- 2 (10.75 oz.) cans Chicken Gumbo Soup
- ¾ c. uncooked instant white rice

Directions:

1. Heat oven to 375°F. In 2-qt. Casserole, mix shrimp, ham, rice, okra, garlic powder, Cajun seasoning, onion, water, and soup.
2. Bake till the gumbo is bubbly and hot for 35 minutes. Mix gumbo; serve.

Nutritional Information:

Calories: 287

Total fat: 12 g

Carbs: 41 g

Fiber: 6 g

Protein: 8 g

15. Ham and Cheese Pasta Casserole

Preparation Time: 15 minutes

Cooking Time: 50 minutes

Servings: 4

Cooking Time: 50 minutes

Ingredients:

- 1 (16 oz.) package of elbow macaroni
- 1 (8 oz.) package of Cheddar cheese, cubed
- 1 c. cubed, cooked ham
- ½ c. mayonnaise
- 1 c. dry bread crumbs

Directions:

1. Set the oven to 350°F (175°C).
2. Place lightly salted water in a large pot and make it boil. Add elbow macaroni to the boiling water and cook for 8 minutes, occasionally stirring, until cooked through yet firm to chew; strain.
3. In a 9x13-inch baking dish, mix mayonnaise, ham, cheddar cheese, and macaroni until well blended.
4. Dust bread crumbs over the macaroni casserole.
5. Place the casserole in the preheated oven and bake for about 25 minutes until the bread crumbs are lightly browned.

Nutritional Information:

Calories: 287

Total fat: 12 g

Carbs: 41 g

Fiber: 6 g

Protein: 8 g

16. Ham and Chicken Casserole

Preparation Time: 15 minutes

Cooking Time: 55 minutes

Servings: 4

Ingredients:

- ¼ tsp. ground black pepper
- 3 oz. shredded Cheddar cheese
- ½ c. uncooked egg noodles
- 2 tbsps. butter
- 1 c. milk
- ¼ c. chopped celery
- ½ c. of cooked, diced ham
- ¼ tsp. salt
- ½ c. of cooked, cubed chicken breast meat
- 1 tsp. paprika
- 2 tbsps. all-purpose flour

Directions:

1. Preheat an oven to the heat of 200°C/400°F; grease a medium baking dish lightly.
2. Boil a saucepan with lightly salted water; in boiling water, cook egg noodles till al dente for 6-8 minutes. Drain.
3. Oil and heat the saucepan; mix flour in, heating till bubbly. Whisk milk in slowly; cook till smooth and thick for 5 minutes, constantly mixing. Take the saucepan off the heat; mix pepper, salt, celery, ham, chicken, and noodles. Put the mixture into the prepped baking dish.
4. In the prepared pre-heated oven, bake for 15 minutes; sprinkle with paprika and cheese. Bake for 5 minutes more; serve hot.

Nutritional Information:

Calories: 208

Fat: 8 g

Carbs: 33.2 g

Protein: 3.6 g

17. Amish Breakfast Casserole

Preparation Time: 15 minutes

Cooking Time: 20 minutes

Servings: 6

Ingredients:

- 1 lb. sliced bacon, diced
- 1 c. chopped onion
- 6 beaten eggs
- 4 c. shredded frozen hashbrowns, thawed
- 2 c. shredded cheddar cheese
- 1 ½ c. cottage cheese
- 1 ¼ c. shredded Swiss cheese

Directions:

1. Preheat the oven to 350°F. With nonstick cooking spray, spray a baking pan that's 9 x 13. Over medium heat, add the bacon and onion in a large skillet.
2. Cook for 8 minutes or until the bacon is crisp. Remove the skillet from the heat and drain the bacon and onions on paper towels.
3. Add the eggs, hashbrowns, cheddar cheese, cottage cheese, and Swiss cheese in a mixing bowl. Stir until combined.
4. Add the bacon and onions to the bowl. Stir until combined and pour into the baking pan.
5. Bake for 35 minutes or until a knife inserted in the center of the casserole comes out clean. Remove from the oven and let the casserole sit for 5 minutes before serving.

Nutritional Information:

Calories: 165

Fat: 5 g

Fiber: 6 g

Carbs: 22 g

Protein: 5 g

18. Eggs Benedict Casserole

Preparation Time: 15 minutes

Cooking Time: 20 minutes

Servings: 4

Ingredients:

- 12 oz. Canadian bacon, chopped
- 6 English muffins, split and cut into 1" pieces
- 8 eggs
- 2 c. whole milk
- 1 tsp. Onion powder
- ¼ tsp. paprika
- 1 ⅔ c. prepared Hollandaise sauc

Directions:

1. With nonstick cooking spray, spray a baking dish that's 9 x 13. Spread half the Canadian bacon in the bottom of the pan. Spread the English muffins over the bacon.
2. Sprinkle the remaining bacon over the top. In a mixing bowl, add the eggs, milk, and onion powder. Whisk until combined and pour over the top of the casserole.
3. Cover the dish with aluminum foil. Refrigerate for at least 8 hours but not more than 12 hours. Remove from the refrigerator and let the casserole sit at room temperature for 30 minutes.
4. Preheat the oven to 375°F. Sprinkle the paprika over the top. Place the aluminum foil back over the dish. Bake for 35 minutes.
5. Remove the aluminum foil from the dish. Bake for 10-15 minutes or until a knife inserted in the center of the casserole comes out clean.
6. Remove from the oven and serve with the Hollandaise sauce.

Nutritional Information:

Calories: 439

Fat: 3.1 g

Carbohydrates: 80.1 g

Protein: 24.9 g

19. Ham Egg Casserole

Preparation Time: 15 minutes

Cooking Time: 60 minutes

Servings: 4

Ingredients:

- 6 oz. rye bread, sliced into cubes
- 6 oz. reduced-sodium ham, chopped
- 1 c. apple, chopped
- 4 oz. cheddar cheese, shredded
- 2 c. nonfat milk
- 6 eggs, beaten
- Pepper to taste
- ½ c. green onions, sliced thinly

Directions:

1. Preheat your oven to 325°F. Spray your baking pan with oil.
2. Then, arrange half of the bread cubes in the baking pan. Top with the apples, ham, and cheese. Sprinkle the remaining bread on top.
3. In a bowl, beat eggs and stir in the milk and pepper. Sprinkle the green onions on top.
4. Bake in the oven for 50 minutes. Let cool for 10 minutes before serving.

Nutritional Information:

Calories: 208

Fat: 8 g

Carbs: 33.2 g

Protein: 3.6 g

20. Ham Enchilada Casserole

Preparation Time: 15 minutes

Cooking Time: 30 minutes

Servings: 4

Ingredients:

- 2 c. cubed cooked ham
- ½ c. chopped green onions
- 10 flour tortillas, 9" size
- 2 c. shredded cheddar cheese
- 1 tbsp. all-purpose flour
- 2 c. half and half cream
- 6 beaten eggs
- ¼ tsp. salt

Directions:

1. In a mixing bowl, add the ham and green onions. Stir until combined.
2. With nonstick cooking spray, spray a baking pan that's 9 x 13. Spoon ¼ cup of ham filling down the center of each flour tortilla.
3. Sprinkle 2 tablespoons of cheddar cheese over the filling in each tortilla. Roll the tortillas up and place them in the baking pan with the seam side down.
4. Add the all-purpose flour, half and half cream, eggs, and salt in a mixing bowl. Stir until combined and pour over the enchiladas.
5. Cover the pan with aluminum foil. Refrigerate for at least 8 hours but not more than 12 hours.
6. Remove the pan from the refrigerator and let the casserole sit at room temperature for 30 minutes.
7. Preheat the oven to 350°F. Bake for 25 minutes. Remove the aluminum foil from the pan. Over the top, sprinkle the remaining cheddar cheese.
8. Bake for 10-15 minutes or until the casserole is set. Remove from the oven and serve.

Nutritional Information:

Calories: 125

Fat: 5 g

Fiber: 4 g

Carbs: 12 g

Protein: 5 g

21. Ranch Chicken and Potato Casserole

Preparation Time: 15 minutes

Cooking Time: 20 minutes

Servings: 4

Ingredients:

- 1 lb. potatoes, red in color and small in size
- A dash of salt, for taste
- 1 chicken, rotisserie variety, fully cooked and finely shredded
- 2 tbsps. of butter, unsalted variety and soft to the touch
- 2 tbsps. of flour, an all-purpose variety
- 2 c. of milk, whole
- A dash of black pepper, for taste
- 4 tbsps. ranch dressing, seasoning variety
- 2 c. cheddar cheese, finely shredded
- ¼ c. scallions, thinly sliced and for Garnish
- ½ c. sour cream

Directions:

1. The first thing that you need to do is fill up a large sized pot with some cold water. Add in a touch of salt and bring your water to a boil over medium to high heat.
2. Add the potatoes once the water is boiling and cook for another 10 to 12 minutes or until they are soft enough to the touch. Once tender, drain your potatoes and rinse them under some running water.
3. Place your potatoes into a large-sized bowl and mash until smooth in consistency. Set aside for later use.
4. Then, preheat your oven to 375°F. While your oven is heating up, remove your chicken from the bones and shred finely using 2 forks. Toss out the bones.
5. Next, use a large-sized pot and place it over medium heat. Add in your reserved chicken dripping along with your soft flour. Stir thoroughly to combine, and add in your flour. Continue to stir over medium heat for the next minute.
6. Add in your milk, a dash of salt, black pepper, and ranch dressing seasoning. Stir to combine and bring your mixture to a boil. Allow to simmer for the next 5 minutes before turning off the heat of your stove.
7. Add in your shredded cheese, shredded chicken, and mashed potatoes. Fold gently until evenly mixed.
8. Transfer this mixture to a medium-sized casserole dish. Top off with your scallions and remaining cheese.
9. Place into your oven to bake it for about 10 to 15 minutes or until your cheese is fully melted.
10. Remove from heat and serve with some sour cream and extra scallions. Serve right away and enjoy.

Nutritional Information:

Calories: 46

Fat: 3.3 g

Carbohydrates: 2.7 g

Protein: 1.6 g

Calories: 410 g

Carbohydrate: 58.1 g

Protein: 12.2 g

22. Hearty Tortilla Casserole

Preparation Time: 15 minutes

Cooking Time: 70 minutes

Servings: 4

Ingredients:

- ¼ c. heavy whipping cream
- 2 tbsps. taco seasoning
- 1 c. shredded Monterey Jack cheese, divided
- ⅓ c. water
- ½ lb. ground beef
- 1 small onion, finely chopped
- 1 jalapeno pepper, seeded and finely chopped
- 1 garlic clove, minced
- 1 tbsp. canola oil
- 1 c. shredded cheddar cheese, divided
- 1 can (16 oz.) of refried beans
- Sour cream and salsa, optional
- ⅛ tsp. salt
- 4 flour tortillas (8 inches)
- 1 can (4 oz.) of chopped green chilies

Directions:

1. Cook beef on medium heat in a skillet till the meat is not pink anymore. Strain. Pour in water and taco seasoning. Let it simmer, while uncovered, for 5 minutes; remove from the heat and put aside.
2. Sauté garlic, jalapeno, and onion in oil in a saucepan for roughly 8 minutes or till becoming softened.
3. Mix in salt and cream. Keep it covered and let simmer for 5 minutes.
4. Spread 3 tbsps. of sauce in one ungreased 8-in. round or square baking dish. Spread roughly 2 teaspoons of sauce over each tortilla; layer with beans, beef mixture, and 2 tablespoons of each kind of cheese. Roll up and place seam-side facing downward in the baking dish. Add the rest of the sauce on top.
5. Bake, while uncovered, at 350°F for 25 minutes. Drizzle with the rest of the cheeses; bake for 5 minutes more. Serve along with sour cream and salsa if you want.

Nutritional Information: Calories: 46, Fat: 3.3 g , Carbohydrate: 2.7 g , Protein: 1.6 g , Calories: 410 , Carbohydrate: 58.1 g , Protein 12.2 g

23. Herbed Beef Vegetable Casserole

Preparation Time: 15 minutes

Cooking Time: 50 minutes

Servings: 4

Ingredients:

- 2 lb. ground beef
- 1 medium eggplant, cubed
- 2 medium zucchinis, cubed
- 1 medium onion, chopped
- 1 medium sweet yellow pepper
- 3 garlic cloves, minced
- 1 can (28 oz.) of stewed tomatoes
- 1 c. cooked rice
- 1 c. shredded cheddar cheese, divided
- ½ c. beef broth
- ½ tsp. each oregano, savory, and thyme
- ½ tsp. salt
- ¼ tsp. pepper

Directions:

1. Cook beef in a Dutch oven over medium heat till not pink anymore; let drain.
2. Put in the garlic, zucchini, yellow pepper, onion, and eggplant; cook till softened. Put in seasonings, broth, a half cup of cheese, rice, and tomatoes; stir thoroughly.
3. Put to a greased 13x9-inch baking dish. Top with the leftover cheese.
4. Bake while uncovered at 350°F for around 30 minutes or till heated through.

Nutritional Information:

Calories: 200

Fat: 13 g

Protein: 5 g

Carbohydrates: 18 g

24. Herbed Garlic Potato Casserole

Preparation Time: 25 minutes

Cooking Time: 60 minutes

Servings: 4

Ingredients:

- 2 lb. potatoes, sliced into wedges
- 3 tbsps. olive oil
- 1 tsp. herb and garlic seasoning
- Pepper to taste
- 1 bulb garlic
- Salt to taste
- 1 c. Greek yogurt
- ¼ c. Parmesan cheese, grated
- ¼ c. parsley, snipped

Directions:

1. Preheat your oven to 325°F. Add the potatoes to a baking pan.
2. Toss in 1 tablespoon of oil. Season with the herb and garlic mix. Toss to coat evenly.
3. Slice the top off the garlic. Drizzle the garlic with the remaining oil. Add the garlic to the pan. Roast for 50 minutes.
4. Squeeze the garlic into the potatoes. Mash the potatoes. Spread it with the yogurt. Sprinkle the cheese and chopped parsley on top before serving.

Nutritional Information:

Calories: 200

Fat: 13 g

Protein: 5 g

Carbohydrates: 18 g

25. Huevos Rancheros Casserole

Preparation Time: 15 minutes

Cooking Time: 30 minutes

Servings: 5

Ingredients:

- 30 oz. package of frozen tater tots
- 12 eggs
- 1 c. whole milk
- 1 ½ tsps. dried oregano, crushed
- 1 ½ tsps. Ground cumin
- ½ tsp. Chili powder
- ¼ tsp. garlic powder
- 2 c. shredded Mexican blend cheese
- 16 oz. jar thick and chunky salsa
- 1 c. sour cream
- Chopped cilantro to taste

Directions:

1. Preheat the oven to 375°F. With nonstick cooking spray, spray a baking pan that's 9 x 13. Spread the tater tots in the bottom of the baking pan.
2. Add the eggs, milk, oregano, cumin, chili powder, and garlic powder in a mixing bowl. Whisk until combined and pour over the tater tots.
3. Bake for 35 minutes or until a knife inserted near the center of the casserole comes out clean. Sprinkle the Mexican cheese blend over the top. Bake for 5 minutes.
4. Remove from the oven and let the casserole sit for 5 minutes. Spread the salsa over the top. Spoon dollops of sour cream over the salsa. Sprinkle cilantro to taste over the top and serve.

Nutritional Information:

Calories: 165

Fat: 5 g

Fiber: 6 g

Carbs: 22 g

Protein: 5 g

26. Italian Brunch Torte Casserole

Preparation Time: 15 minutes

Cooking Time: 30 minutes

Servings: 4

Ingredients:

- 2 cans of refrigerated crescent rolls, 8 ct. size
- 1 tsp. olive oil
- 6 oz. package of fresh baby spinach
- 1 c. sliced fresh mushrooms
- 7 eggs
- 1 c. grated Parmesan cheese
- 2 tsps. dried Italian seasoning
- ⅛ tsp. black pepper
- 8 oz. thinly sliced deli ham
- 8 oz. sliced hard salami
- 8 oz. sliced provolone cheese
- 2 jars of roasted red bell peppers, 12 oz. size

Directions:

1. Preheat the oven to 350°F. Spray an 8" springform pan with nonstick cooking spray. Cut an 18" square of heavy-duty aluminum foil. Wrap the foil around the outside of the pan.
2. Remove the crescent dough from one can of crescent rolls. Press the dough in the bottom of the springform pan to form a crust. Bake for 10-12 minutes or until the crust is set.
3. Remove the pan from the oven. While the crust is baking, add the olive oil to a skillet over medium heat. When the oil is hot, add the spinach and mushrooms. Saute for 5 minutes.
4. Remove the skillet from the heat and drain off all the liquid. Pat the spinach and mushrooms with paper towels to remove the moisture.
5. Add 6 eggs, Parmesan cheese, Italian seasoning, and black pepper in a mixing bowl. Whisk until combined. Place half the ham over the crust in the pan. Place half the salami over the ham.
6. Place half the provolone cheese over the salami. Drain the liquid from the red peppers. Slice the peppers and dry them with paper towels to remove the moisture.
7. Place half the peppers over the cheese. Pour half the eggs over the top. Repeat the layering steps one more time.
8. Remove the dough from the remaining crescent rolls. Separate the dough into triangles and place them over the top. Place them as close together as possible.
9. In a small bowl, add 1 egg. Whisk until combined and brush over the crescent rolls. Bake for 1 hour or until the casserole is set in the center. If the top is browning too fast, loosely cover the top with aluminum foil.

10. Remove from the oven and run a knife around the edges of the pan to loosen the casserole from the pan. Let the casserole sit for 15 minutes. Remove the casserole from the pan and serve.

Nutritional Information:

Calories: 388

Fat: 12.8 g

Carbohydrates: 54.8 g

Protein: 17.3 g

27. Roasted Pepper and Sourdough Brunch Casserole

Preparation Time: 15 minutes

Cooking Time: 30 minutes

Servings: 4

Ingredients:

- 3 c. sourdough bread, cubed
- 12 oz. jar of roasted red pepper strips, drained
- 1 c. shredded sharp cheddar cheese
- 1 c. shredded Monterey Jack cheese
- 1 c. cottage cheese
- 6 eggs
- 1 c. whole milk
- ¼ c. chopped fresh cilantro
- ¼ tsp. black pepper

Directions:

1. With nonstick cooking spray, spray a baking pan that's 11 x 7. Place the bread cubes in the baking pan.
2. Spread the red pepper strips, cheddar cheese, and Monterey Jack cheese over the bread.
3. In a blender, add the cottage cheese. Process until smooth. Add the eggs and milk to the blender.
4. Process until well combined and pour over the bread cubes. Sprinkle the cilantro and black pepper over the top.
5. Cover the pan with plastic wrap. Refrigerate for at least 8 hours but not more than 12 hours. Remove from the refrigerator and remove the plastic wrap.
6. Preheat the oven to 375°F. Bake for 40 minutes or until the casserole is set in the center. Remove from the oven and let the casserole sit for 5 minutes before serving.

Nutritional Information:

Calories: 153

Fat: 9 g

Carbohydrates: 10 g

Protein: 9 g

28. Sausage Biscuit and Blueberry Casserole

Preparation Time: 15 minutes

Cooking Time: 30 minutes

Servings: 4

Ingredients:

- 2 c. Bisquick
- ½ c. whole milk
- 1 egg
- 1 tsp. vanilla extract
- 1 c. fresh or frozen blueberries
- 6 cooked breakfast sausage links, chopped
- Maple syrup to taste

Directions:

1. Preheat the oven to 350°F. Spray an 8" square baking pan with nonstick cooking spray. Add the Bisquick, milk, egg, and vanilla extract in a mixing bowl. Whisk until combined.
2. Fold in the blueberries. Spread the batter in the pan. Sprinkle the sausages over the top.
3. For 20 minutes or until set and lightly browned, bake the casserole. Remove from the oven and serve with maple syrup to taste.

Nutritional Information:

Calories: 388

Fat: 12.8 g

Carbohydrates: 54.8 g

Protein: 17.3 g

29. Sausage Garlic Bread Breakfast Casserole

Preparation Time: 15 minutes

Cooking Time: 30 minutes

Servings: 4

Ingredients:

- 1 lb. ground pork sausage
- 1 large green bell pepper, chopped
- 1 c. chopped onion
- 1 lb. loaf garlic cheese bread, cubed
- 1 c. shredded cheddar cheese
- 6 eggs
- 2 c. whole milk
- 1 tsp. dry mustard

Directions:

1. Over medium heat, add the sausage, green bell pepper, and onion in a large skillet. Stir frequently to break the sausage into crumbles as it cooks.
2. Cook for 8 minutes or until the sausage is browned and no longer pink. Remove the skillet from the heat and drain off all the excess grease.
3. With nonstick cooking spray, spray a baking pan that's 9 x 13. Place the garlic bread cubes in the bottom of the baking pan. Spoon the sausage over the top. Sprinkle the cheddar cheese over the sausage. In a mixing bowl, add the eggs, milk, and dry mustard.
4. Whisk until combined and pour over the top of the casserole. Make sure the bread is coated in the eggs.
5. Cover the pan with plastic wrap. Refrigerate for at least 8 hours but not more than 12 hours. Remove from the refrigerator and let the casserole sit at room temperature for 30 minutes.
6. Preheat the oven to 350°F. Remove the plastic wrap from the pan. For 30 minutes or until set in the center, bake the casserole. Take it out of the oven and cool it for 5 minutes before cutting.

Nutritional Information:

Calories: 125

Fat: 5 g

Fiber: 4 g

Carbs: 12 g

Protein: 5 g

30. Sausage Stuffing Breakfast Casserole

Preparation Time: 15 minutes

Cooking Time: 30 minutes

Servings: 4

Ingredients:

- 1 lb. ground pork sausage
- 1 tsp. Dried Italian seasoning
- ½ tsp. salt
- 6 eggs
- 2 c. whole milk
- ½ c. dry Cream of Wheat cereal
- 1 tsp. Tabasco sauce
- 4 c. cubed bread stuffing
- 2 c. shredded cheddar cheese

Directions:

1. Over medium heat, add the sausage to a skillet. Stir frequently to break the sausage into crumbles as it cooks. Cook for 8 minutes or until the sausage is well-browned and no longer pink.
2. Remove the skillet from the heat and drain off the excess grease. Sprinkle the Italian seasoning and salt over the sausage. Stir until combined.
3. Add the eggs, milk, Cream of Wheat, and Tabasco sauce in a mixing bowl. Whisk until well combined. Add the bread stuffing and sausage to the bowl. Toss until combined.
4. With nonstick cooking spray, spray a baking pan that's 9 x 13. Spoon the casserole into the pan. Cover the pan with aluminum foil. Refrigerate for at least 8 hours but not more than 12 hours.
5. Preheat the oven to 350°F. Remove the casserole from the refrigerator and remove the aluminum foil. Sprinkle the cheddar cheese over the top. Place the aluminum foil back over the pan.
6. Bake for 30 minutes. Remove the aluminum foil from the pan. Bake for 15 minutes or until the casserole is set in the center and lightly browned. Remove from the oven and serve.

Nutritional Information:

Calories: 95

Fat: 7 g

Carbohydrates: 4 g

Protein: 1 g

31. Ham Vegetable Strata

Preparation Time: 15 minutes

Cooking Time: 30 minutes

Servings: 4

Ingredients:

- 1 small zucchini, cut into ½" slices
- 2 c. fresh broccoli florets
- ½ c. shredded carrot
- 12 slices of bread, crust removed
- 1 c. cubed cooked ham
- 8 oz. can of sliced mushrooms, drained
- 1 c. shredded sharp cheddar cheese
- 1 c. shredded Swiss cheese
- 12 eggs
- 2 ½ c. whole milk
- ¼ c. chopped onion
- ½ tsp. ground mustard
- ¼ tsp. salt
- ⅛ tsp. black pepper
- 1 ½ c. crushed cornflakes
- ¼ c. melted unsalted butter

Directions:

1. Add 1" of water to a saucepan over medium heat. Add the zucchini, broccoli, and carrot to the pan. Bring to a boil and place a lid on the pan.
2. Cook for 5-6 minutes or until the vegetables are tender. Remove the pan from the heat and drain all the water from the pan.
3. Cut each bread slice in half. With nonstick cooking spray, spray a baking pan that's 9 x 13. Place half the bread slices in the bottom of the pan. Spoon half the cooked vegetables, ½ cup of ham, half the mushrooms, ½ cup of cheddar cheese, and ½ cup of Swiss cheese over the bread.
4. Place the remaining bread slices over the top. Spoon the remaining vegetables, ham, mushrooms, cheddar cheese, and Swiss cheese over the bread.
5. Add the eggs, milk, onion, ground mustard, salt, and black pepper in a mixing bowl. Whisk until combined and pour over the top of the casserole. Do not stir. Cover the pan with plastic wrap. Refrigerate for at least 8 hours but not more than 12 hours.
6. Remove the pan from the refrigerator and let it sit at room temperature for 30 minutes. Preheat the oven to 350°D. Remove the plastic wrap from the pan. Sprinkle the cornflakes over the top. Drizzle the melted butter over the cornflakes.

7. Bake for 45-50 minutes or until a knife inserted in the center comes out clean. Take out of the oven and cool for 5 minutes before serving.

Nutritional Information:

Calories: 278

Fat: 2.9 g

Carbs: 59 g

Protein: 6.6 g

32. Italian Apricot Pancetta Strata

Preparation Time: 10 minutes

Cooking Time: 30 minutes

Servings: 4

Ingredients:

- 5 oz. pancetta, finely chopped
- 2 tbsps. unsalted butter
- 1 ⅓ c. finely chopped onion
- 2 c. sliced fresh mushrooms
- 3 c. fresh baby spinach, chopped
- 5 c. cubed whole grain bread
- 6 eggs
- 1 c. heavy whipping cream
- ¼ tsp. Salt
- ¼ tsp. black pepper
- 8 oz. carton mascarpone cheese
- 1 c. shredded mozzarella cheese
- ½ c. shredded Asiago cheese
- 1 c. apricot preserves
- 3 tbsps. Minced fresh basil

Directions:

1. Over medium heat, add the pancetta to a large skillet. Saute for 5 minutes or until the pancetta is crisp. Remove the pancetta from the skillet with a slotted spoon and drain on paper towels. Drain off all but 1 tablespoon of drippings in the skillet.
2. To the skillet, add 1 tablespoon of butter. When the butter melts, add the onion. Saute for 5 minutes. Remove the onion from the skillet and spoon it into a bowl.
3. To the skillet, add 1 tablespoon of butter. When the butter melts, add the mushrooms. Saute for 4 minutes. Add the spinach to the skillet. Saute for 2 minutes. Remove the skillet from the heat and spoon into the bowl with the onions.
4. Add the bread cubes and pancetta to the bowl. Toss until combined. With nonstick cooking spray, spray a baking pan that's 9 x 13. Spread the bread and vegetables in the pan. Add the eggs, heavy whipping cream, salt, and black pepper in a mixing bowl. Whisk until combined. Add the mascarpone cheese to the bowl. Stir until combined and pour over the bread in the pan.
5. Sprinkle the mozzarella and Asiago cheese over the top. Spread the apricot preserves over the cheese. Cover the baking pan with aluminum foil. Refrigerate for at least 8 hours but not more than 24 hours. Remove from the refrigerator and let sit for 15 minutes at room temperature before baking. Remove the aluminum foil from the pan

6. Preheat the oven to 350°F. Bake for 35-45 minutes or until the strata are done in the center and golden brown. Remove from the oven and sprinkle the basil over the top. Let the strata rest for 5 minutes before serving.

Nutritional Information:

Calories: 278

Fat: 2.9 g

Carbs: 59 g

Protein: 6.6 g

33. Goat Cheese, Artichokes, and Ham Strata

Preparation Time: 15 minutes

Cooking Time: 35 minutes

Servings: 4

Ingredients:

- 2 c. whole milk
- 2 tbsps. olive oil
- 1 lb. loaf sourdough bread, cut into 1" cubes
- 5 eggs
- 1 ½ c. half and half cream
- 1 tbsp. minced garlic
- 1 ½ tsps. herbes de Provence
- ¾ tsp. Black pepper
- ½ tsp. Ground nutmeg
- ½ tsp. Crushed dried sage
- ½ tsp. crushed dried oregano
- 8 oz. crumbled goat cheese
- 12 oz. smoked cooked ham, chopped
- 3 jars of marinated artichoke hearts, 6 oz. size
- 1 ½ c. shredded Parmesan cheese
- 1 c. shredded fontina cheese

Directions:

1. With nonstick cooking spray, spray a baking pan that's 9 x 13. In a large mixing bowl, add the milk and olive oil. Whisk until combined.
2. Add the bread cubes to the bowl. Toss until the bread cubes are coated in the liquids. Let the bread sit for 10 minutes.
3. Add the eggs, half-and-half cream, garlic, herbes de Provence, black pepper, nutmeg, sage, and oregano in a separate mixing bowl. Whisk until combined. Add the goat cheese and stir until combined.
4. Spread half the bread cubes in the baking pan. Sprinkle half the ham over the bread cubes. Drain the artichokes and cut them in half lengthwise. Spread half the artichokes over the bread. Sprinkle ¾ cup of Parmesan cheese and ½ cup of fontina cheese over the top.
5. Repeat the layering steps using the remaining bread cubes, ham, artichokes, Parmesan, and fontina cheese. Pour the eggs over the top. Do not stir. Cover the pan with plastic wrap. Refrigerate for at least 2 hours but not longer than 12 hours.
6. Remove the pan from the refrigerator and remove the plastic wrap. Preheat the oven to 350°F. Bake for 1 hour or until the center of the strata is set and the edges browned. Remove from the oven and let sit for 10 minutes before serving.

Nutritional Information:

Calories: 278

Fat: 2.9 g

Carbs: 59 g

Protein: 6.6 g

34. Ham Enchilada Breakfast Bake

Preparation Time: 15 minutes

Cooking Time: 30 minutes

Servings: 4

Ingredients:

- 2 c. chopped shaved deli ham
- ½ c. chopped green onion
- ½ c. chopped green bell pepper
- 10 oz. package of frozen spinach, thawed and patted dry
- 4 oz. can dice green chiles, drained
- 1 ¼ c. shredded cheddar cheese
- 1 ¼ c. shredded Monterey Jack cheese
- 8 flour tortillas, 6" size
- 6 beaten eggs
- 2 ½ c. half and half cream
- 2 tbsps. all-purpose flour
- ¼ tsp. garlic powder
- ¼ tsp. salt
- 3 drops of Tabasco sauce

Directions:

1. Preheat the oven to 350°. With nonstick cooking spray, spray a baking pan that's 9 x 13. Add the ham, green onion, bell pepper, spinach, and green chiles in a mixing bowl. Stir until combined.
2. In a separate bowl, add the cheddar cheese and Monterey Jack cheese. Stir until combined. Spoon ¼ cup of ham filling down the center of each tortilla.
3. Sprinkle 2 tablespoons of cheese mixture over the filling. Roll the tortillas up. Place the enchiladas, seam side down, in the baking pan.
4. Add the eggs, half and half cream, all-purpose flour, garlic powder, salt, and Tabasco sauce in a mixing bowl. Whisk until combined and pour over the enchiladas. Sprinkle the remaining ham filling over the top.
5. Cover the pan with aluminum foil. Bake for 50 minutes. Remove the aluminum foil from the pan. Sprinkle the remaining cheeses over the top.
6. Bake for 5 minutes or until the cheese melts. Remove from the oven and serve.

Nutritional Information: Calories: 151, Fat: 2 g, Fiber: 6 g, Carbs: 12 g, Protein: 4 g

35. Ham Tortilla Breakfast Casserole

Preparation Time: 15 minutes

Cooking Time: 40 minutes

Servings: 4

Ingredients:

- 1 c. sliced fresh mushrooms
- 1 c. chopped onion
- ½ chopped green bell pepper
- ¼ c. unsalted butter, cubed
- 6 beaten eggs
- ¼ c. whole milk
- ¼ tsp. black pepper
- 1 c. cubed cooked ham
- 10.75 oz. can cream of mushroom soup
- 10 warm flour tortillas, 8" size
- 1 ½ c. shredded cheddar cheese

Directions:

1. In a large skillet over medium heat, add the mushrooms, onion, green bell pepper, and butter. Saute for 5 minutes or until the vegetables are tender.
2. Add the eggs, milk, black pepper, and ham in a mixing bowl. Whisk until combined and add to the skillet.
3. Stir constantly and cook for about 4-5 minutes or until the eggs are set. Remove the skillet from the heat. With nonstick cooking spray, spray a baking pan that's 9 x 13.
4. Spread half the cream of mushroom soup in the bottom of the pan. Spread 3 tablespoons of egg filling down the center of each tortilla.
5. Sprinkle 1 tablespoon of cheddar cheese over the egg filling in each tortilla. Roll the tortillas up and place them with the seam side down in the baking dish.
6. Spread the remaining cream of mushroom soup over the top of the tortillas. Sprinkle the remaining cheddar cheese over the soup. Preheat the oven to 350°F.
7. Bake for 20 minutes or until the casserole is hot and bubbly. Remove from the oven and serve.

Nutritional Information: Calories: 191, Total Fat: 10 g, Saturated Fat: 3 g , Cholesterol: 15 mg , Carbohydrates: 14 g , Fiber: 14 g , Protein: 12 g , Phosphorus: 189 mg , Potassium: 327 mg , Sodium: 40 mg

36. Ham, Mushroom and Cheese Casserole

Preparation Time: 15 minutes

Cooking Time: 30 minutes

Servings: 4

Ingredients:

- 1 ½ c. shredded cheddar cheese
- 1 ½ c. shredded mozzarella cheese
- 2 tbsps. unsalted butter
- 8 oz. fresh sliced mushrooms
- 1 red bell pepper, chopped
- 6 green onions, chopped
- 1 ¾ c. cubed cooked ham
- 8 eggs
- 1 ¾ c. whole milk
- ¼ c. all-purpose flour
- ¼ tsp. salt
- ¼ tsp. black pepper

Directions:

1. With nonstick cooking spray, spray a baking pan that's 9 x 13. Spread the cheddar and mozzarella cheese in the bottom of the pan. In a skillet over medium heat, add the butter.
2. When the butter melts, add the mushrooms, red bell pepper, and green onions. Saute for 6 minutes or until the vegetables are tender.
3. Remove the skillet from the heat and stir the ham into the vegetables. Spread over the cheeses in the baking pan.
4. Add the eggs, milk, all-purpose flour, salt, and black pepper in a mixing bowl. Whisk until combined and pour over the top of the vegetables. Cover the pan with plastic wrap. Refrigerate for at least 8 hours but not more than 12 hours.
5. Remove from the refrigerator and remove the plastic wrap. Let the casserole sit for 30 minutes at room temperature.
6. Bake for 35-45 minutes or until a knife inserted in the center of the casserole comes out clean. Remove from the oven and cool for 5 minutes before serving.

Nutritional Information: Calories: 191, Total Fat: 10 g, Saturated Fat: 3 g, Cholesterol: 15 mg, Carbohydrates: 14 g, Fiber: 14 g , Protein: 12 g , Phosphorus: 189 mg , Potassium: 327 mg , Sodium: 40 mg

37. Two Cheese Ham Souffle Bake

Preparation Time: 15 minutes

Cooking Time: 30 minutes

Servings: 4

Ingredients:

- 16 slices of day-old bread, crust removed and cubed
- 1 lb. cooked ham, cubed
- 2 c. shredded cheddar cheese
- 1 c. shredded Swiss cheese
- 6 beaten eggs
- 3 c. whole milk
- ½ tsp. Onion powder
- ½ tsp. Ground mustard
- ⅛ tsp. black pepper
- A pinch of cayenne pepper
- 1 ½ c. finely crushed cornflakes
- 3 tbsps. Melted unsalted butter

Directions:

1. With nonstick cooking spray, spray a baking pan that's 9 x 13. Spread half the bread cubes in the bottom of the pan.
2. Sprinkle the ham, cheddar, and Swiss cheese over the bread cubes. Sprinkle the remaining bread cubes over the top.
3. Add the eggs, milk, onion, powder, ground mustard, black pepper, and cayenne in a mixing bowl. Whisk until combined and pour over the top of the bread. Cover the pan with plastic wrap. Refrigerate for at least 8 hours but not more than 12 hours.
4. Remove the casserole from the refrigerator and remove the plastic wrap. Let the casserole sit for 30 minutes at room temperature.
5. Preheat the oven to 375°F. Sprinkle the cornflakes over the top of the casserole. Drizzle the butter over the cornflakes.
6. Bake for 40 minutes or until a knife inserted in the center of the casserole comes out clean. Remove from the oven and let the casserole rest for 10 minutes before serving.

Nutritional Information: Calories: 68, Fat: 5.1 g, Fiber: 0.5 g, Carbs: 1.3 g, Protein: 4.6 g

38. Ham Broccoli Brunch Casserole

Preparation Time: 15 minutes

Cooking Time: 30 minutes

Servings: 4

Ingredients:

- 8 oz. loaf day old French bread, cubed
- ½ c. melted unsalted butter
- 2 c. shredded cheddar cheese
- 2 c. chopped frozen broccoli, thawed
- 2 c. cubed cooked ham
- 4 beaten eggs
- 2 c. whole milk
- ¼ tsp. black pepper

Directions:

1. With nonstick cooking spray, spray a baking pan that's 9 x 13. Add the bread and butter to a mixing bowl. Toss until the bread cubes are coated in the butter.
2. Spread half the bread cubes in the bottom of the pan. Sprinkle 1 cup of cheddar cheese, 1 cup of broccoli, and 1 cup of ham over the bread cubes. Repeat the layering steps using the remaining bread, cheddar cheese, broccoli, and ham.
3. In a mixing bowl, add the eggs, milk, and black pepper. Whisk until combined and pour over the top of the casserole.
4. Cover the pan with aluminum foil. Refrigerate for at least 8 hours but not more than 12 hours.
5. Remove the casserole from the refrigerator and remove the aluminum foil. Let the casserole sit for 30 minutes at room temperature. Preheat the oven to 350°F.
6. Bake for 35-40 minutes or until a knife inserted near the center of the casserole comes out clean. Remove from the oven and let the casserole rest for 5 minutes before serving.

Nutritional Information:

Calories: 151

Fat: 2 g

Fiber: 6 g

Carbs: 12 g

Protein: 4 g

39. Cheesy Breakfast Ham Casserole

Preparation Time: 15 minutes

Cooking Time: 30 minutes

Servings: 4

Ingredients:

- 5 c. cubed bread
- 2 c. cubed cooked ham
- ¼ c. chopped green bell pepper
- 2 tbsps. chopped onion
- 2 c. shredded cheddar cheese
- 1 c. shredded Pepper Jack cheese
- 10.75 oz. can cream of chicken soup
- 1 ⅓ c. whole milk
- 4 beaten eggs
- 1 c. mayonnaise
- ½ tsp. black pepper
- A pinch of cayenne pepper
- 2 tbsps. melted unsalted butter
- 2 tbsps. minced fresh parsley

Directions:

1. With nonstick cooking spray, spray a baking pan that's 9 x 13. Spread 3 ½ cups of bread cubes in the bottom of the pan. Sprinkle the ham, green bell pepper, onion, cheddar cheese, and Pepper Jack cheese over the bread cubes.
2. In a mixing bowl, add the cream of chicken soup and milk. Whisk until combined. Add the eggs, mayonnaise, black pepper, and cayenne pepper.
3. Whisk until combined and pour over the top of the casserole. Cover the pan with aluminum foil. Refrigerate for at least 8 hours but not more than 12 hours.
4. Remove the casserole from the refrigerator. Remove the aluminum foil. Let the casserole sit for 30 minutes at room temperature. Preheat the oven to 350°F.
5. Add 1 ½ cups of bread cubes and butter in a mixing bowl. Toss until the bread cubes are coated in the butter. Sprinkle the bread cubes over the top of the casserole. Bake for 40-45 minutes or until a knife inserted in the center of the casserole comes out clean.
6. Remove from the oven and sprinkle the parsley over the top. Let the casserole sit for 5 minutes before serving.

Chapter 3:
Meat (Beef, Turkey, Chicken, Pork, and Lamb) Recipes

40. Beef Wild Rice Casserole

Preparation Time: 15 minutes

Cooking Time: 30 minutes

Servings: 4

Ingredients:

- 1 lb. ground beef
- 2 c. wild rice, uncooked
- 8 oz. bacon, diced
- 1 c. celery, chopped
- 1 c. onion, chopped
- 1 green bell pepper, chopped
- 1 tsp. salt
- ½ tsp. black pepper
- 10.75 oz. can cream of mushroom soup
- ⅛ tsp. dried marjoram
- 3 qt. boiling water

Directions:

1. Wash the wild rice and let it soak in water for 2 hours. The rice needs to have about 4" of cold water above the rice. In a skillet over medium heat, add the bacon.
2. Cook the bacon until done and crispy. Remove the bacon from the skillet and drain on paper towels. Leave the bacon drippings in the skillet.
3. Add the ground beef, onion, celery, green bell pepper, salt, black pepper, and marjoram to the skillet. Stir frequently, breaking the ground beef into crumbles as it cooks.
4. Cook for about 7 minutes or until the vegetables are tender and the ground beef is done and well browned. Drain off the excess grease.
5. In a large saucepan over medium-low heat, add the boiling water. Add the rice and cook until the rice is at a full boil. Turn the heat off and cover the saucepan with a lid.
6. Let the rice sit for 10 minutes. Drain the rice and add the rice to the skillet with the vegetables and ground beef.
7. Preheat the oven to 350°F. Spray a 3-quart casserole dish with nonstick cooking spray. Add the rice mixture from the skillet along with the can of cream of mushroom soup.
8. Stir until well combined. Cover the dish with a lid or aluminum foil. Bake for 1 hour or until the rice is done and the casserole is bubbly.
9. Sprinkle the bacon over the top of the casserole and bake for 5 minutes. Remove the dish from the oven and serve.

Nutritional Information: Calories: 121, Fat: 8 g, Carbohydrates: 5 g, Protein: 4 g

41. Wild Rice Stuffing

Preparation Time: 15 minutes

Cooking Time: 30 minutes

Servings: 4

Ingredients:

- 2 c. wild rice
- 1 large onion, minced
- 1 c. finely diced celery
- 4 c. chicken broth
- ¼ tsp. salt
- 1 c. chopped walnuts
- 1 c. chopped mushrooms
- ½ tsp. Celery salt
- ½ tsp. Poultry seasoning
- ⅓ c. + 1 tbsp. unsalted butter

Directions:

1. Add the rice and ⅓ cup of butter in a saucepan over medium heat. Stir constantly until the rice is lightly browned. Stir in the onion and celery. Cook for 3 minutes.
2. Stir in the chicken broth, rice, and salt. Bring the rice to a boil and reduce the heat to medium-low. Place a lid on the saucepan. Simmer for 30 minutes.
3. In a skillet over medium heat, add 1 tablespoon of butter, walnuts, and mushrooms. Saute for 5 minutes.
4. Add the mixture to the saucepan with the rice. Stir in the celery salt and poultry seasoning. Cook for 1 minute. Remove the rice from the heat and serve.

Nutritional Information:

Calories: 121

Fat: 8 g

Carbohydrates: 5 g

Protein: 4 g

42. Chicken Flavored Rice

Preparation Time: 15 minutes

Cooking Time: 30 minutes

Servings: 4

Ingredients:

- 1 ½ c. uncooked instant rice
- 1 ½ c. hot water
- ¼ c. unsalted butter
- ¼ c. chopped green onion
- 2 tsps. chicken bouillon granules
- ¼ tsp. Dried basil
- ⅛ tsp. garlic powder
- 4 oz. can sliced mushrooms, drained
- 1 tbsp. minced fresh parsley
- 1 tbsp. Grated Parmesan cheese

Directions:

1. In a saucepan over medium heat, add the instant rice, water, butter, green onion, chicken bouillon granules, basil, and garlic powder. Place a lid on the pan and bring the rice to a boil. Simmer for about 5 minutes.
2. Stir in the mushrooms and cook for about 5 minutes or until the rice is tender. Remove the pan from the heat and stir in the parsley and Parmesan cheese.
3. Place the lid back on the pan and let the rice sit for 5 minutes before serving. Fluff the rice with a fork before serving.

Nutritional Information:

Calories: 49

Fat: 1.9 g

Carbohydrates: 7 g

Protein: 3 g

43. Chicken Tetrazzini

Preparation Time: 15 minutes

Cooking Time: 30 minutes

Servings: 4 minutes

Ingredients:

- 10 oz. dry linguine, cooked
- 2 tbsps. butter
- ¼ c. all-purpose flour
- 2 ½ c. chicken stock
- 1 ½ c. milk
- ½ c. grated Parmesan cheese, divided
- 1 oz. reduced-fat cream cheese
- Salt and pepper to taste
- 4 tsps. olive oil, divided
- 1 lb. mushrooms, sliced
- 1 medium onion, chopped
- 5 cloves garlic, minced
- 1 tsp. thyme
- 1 tsp. marjoram
- ½ tsp. tarragon
- ½ c. white wine
- 3 c. rotisserie chicken, shredded
- 1 c. frozen mixed vegetables
- Cooking spray
- 2 c. bread crumbs
- ¼ c. fresh parsley, chopped

Directions:

1. Preheat the oven to 375°F and prepare a 9x13" baking dish with cooking spray.
2. Melt the butter in a medium saucepan over medium heat. Stir in the flour and cook for 2 minutes, whisking constantly.
3. Gradually add the stock and milk and bring it to a boil. Reduce the heat, and simmer for 5 minutes.
4. Stir in half the Parmesan cheese, cream cheese, salt, and pepper. Remove the pan from the heat and set it aside.
5. Heat a large skillet over medium-high heat. Add 1 tablespoon of olive oil to the pan; swirl to coat. Add mushrooms and sauté for 3 minutes, stirring occasionally. Add the onion, garlic, thyme, marjoram, and tarragon, and combine well.

6. Add the wine, stir, and cook for 1 minute.
7. Combine the cheese sauce, mushroom mixture, pasta, chicken, and vegetables. Spoon it into the prepared pan.
8. Combine the bread crumbs with the remaining Parmesan, and sprinkle it over the casserole.
9. Bake at 375°F for 30 minutes or until browned and bubbly. Top with parsley.

Nutritional Information:

Calories: 435

Fat: 12 g

Carbs: 45 g

Protein: 33 g

Sodium: 573 mg

44. Chicken Tamale Casserole

Preparation Time: 15 minutes

Cooking Time: 50 minutes

Servings: 4

Ingredients:

- 1 c. Mexican blend shredded cheese, divided
- ½ c. milk
- 1 egg
- ½ tsp. ground cumin
- ½ tsp. chili powder
- ⅛ tsp. ground red pepper
- 1 clove of garlic, minced
- 1 ½ c. cream-style corn
- 1 (8 ½ oz.) box of corn muffin mix
- 1 (4 oz.) can of chopped green chilies, drained
- 1 ½ c. red enchilada sauce (such as Old El Paso)
- 2 c. shredded rotisserie chicken
- ½ c. sour cream
- ½ c. cilantro, chopped
- Cooking spray

Directions:

1. Preheat the oven to 400°F and prepare a 9x13" baking dish with cooking spray.
2. In a large mixing bowl, combine ¼ cup of cheese with the milk, egg, cumin, chili powder, red pepper, garlic, corn, muffin mix, and green chilies. Stir just to combine.
3. Bake for 15 minutes or until it is set. Pierce the entire surface liberally with a fork and pour the enchilada sauce over the top.
4. Top with chicken, and sprinkle with the remaining ¾ cup of cheese.
5. Bake for another 15 minutes or until the cheese is melted.
6. Remove the casserole from the oven and let it stand for 5 minutes.
7. Cut it into 8 pieces. Top each serving with 1 tablespoon of sour cream and garnish with cilantro.

Nutritional Information: Calories: 354, Fat: 14 g, Carbs: 36 g, Protein: 19 g, Sodium: 620 mg

45. Mom's Creamy Chicken and Broccoli Casserole

Preparation Time: 15 minutes

Cooking Time: 30 minutes

Servings: 4

Ingredients:

- 2 c. broccoli florets
- 1 tbsp. vegetable oil
- 1 c. onion, diced
- 1 lb. mushrooms, sliced
- 2 cloves garlic, crushed and minced
- 1 stalk of celery, diced
- 3 tbsps. all-purpose flour
- 1 ½ c. milk
- 1 tsp. rubbed sage
- 3 c. skinless rotisserie chicken, chopped
- ½ c. plain fat-free Greek yogurt
- ¼ c. mayonnaise
- Salt and pepper to taste
- ½ Swiss cheese, shredded
- ¼ c. Parmesan cheese, grated

Directions:

1. Preheat the broiler. In a small saucepan, boil 2 inches of water and steam the broccoli. Remove it from the heat promptly and drain the water.
2. Place a large, ovenproof skillet over medium-high heat. Heat the oil, and add the onion, mushrooms, garlic, and celery. Cook for 10 minutes until the mushrooms brown and the liquid evaporates, stirring occasionally.
3. Sprinkle the flour over the vegetables and stir for 1 minute. Add the milk and sage.
4. Bring it to a boil, and cook for 3 minutes or until it is thick and bubbly.
5. Stir in the broccoli and chicken and cook to heat through.
6. Remove the pan from the heat. Add the yogurt, mayonnaise, salt, and pepper. Top with the cheese and broil for 2 minutes.

Nutritional Information: Calories: 277, Fat: 13 g, Carbs: 15 g, Protein: 29 g, Sodium: 547 mg

46. Baked Chicken and Sweet Potato Enchilada

Preparation Time: 15 minutes

Cooking Time: 30 minutes

Servings: 4

Ingredients:

- 1 c. barbecue sauce of choice
- 1 ½ c. enchilada sauce
- 1 lb. boneless skinless chicken breasts
- 2 tsps. butter
- ½ small red onion, diced
- 2 cloves garlic, minced
- 2 medium sweet potatoes, cooked and diced
- ½ c. corn kernels
- ½ tsp. cumin
- ½ tsp. chili powder
- 9 (6-inch) corn tortillas
- ½ c. pepper jack cheese, shredded
- ½ c. mozzarella, shredded
- ½ c. cilantro, chopped
- For the topping: avocado and sour cream, if desired

Directions:

1. Preheat the oven to 375°F and coat a 9x13" baking dish with cooking spray. Whisk the barbecue and enchilada sauce together in a large bowl.
2. Arrange the chicken breasts in the baking pan, and drizzle ¼ c. of sauce. Bake for 20–25 minutes, or until juices run clear and chicken is no longer pink.
3. Remove the pan from the oven and allow the chicken to cool for a few minutes. Remove the chicken from the pan and shred it with forks. Set it aside, together with the cooking liquids.
4. Wipe out the pan and coat it once more with cooking spray. Meanwhile, melt the butter in a large skillet over medium-high heat. Add the onion and garlic and cook for a few minutes.
5. Add 1 cup of the enchilada sauce, diced sweet potatoes, corn, cumin, and chili powder. Stir to combine, and then add it to the chicken mixture in the baking pan.
6. Place the remaining barbecue-enchilada sauce on a large plate. One at a time, dip 3 corn tortillas in the sauce (coating both sides) and arrange them in the baking dish, cutting one to fit, if necessary, to completely cover the bottom.
7. Place half the chicken and sweet potato mixture on top of the tortillas. Cover with ¼ cup of cheese and about ¼ cup of enchilada sauce. Repeat the layers once, and top with the remaining tortillas, sauce, and cheese.

8. Cover with foil and bake for 30–40 minutes, or until the enchiladas are warmed and the cheese is completely melted. Cool for a few minutes, garnish with cilantro, and then serve with sour cream and avocado if desired.

Nutritional Information:

Calories: 276

Fat: 8 g

Carbs: 38 g

Protein: 18 g

Sodium: 745 mg

47. Chicken Mushroom and Potato Bake

Preparation Time: 15 minutes

Cooking Time: 60 minutes

Servings: 4

Ingredients:

- 6 strips of bacon, chopped
- 1 small onion, diced
- 3 lb. potatoes, peeled and sliced ⅛" thick
- 8 oz. chicken breast, cut into 1-inch pieces
- 8 oz. mushrooms, quartered
- Salt and pepper, to taste
- Onion powder
- ⅓ c. cheddar, shredded
- ½ c. chicken stock
- ¼ c. cream
- ¼ c. chopped green onion
- ½ c. Italian parsley, chopped, to garnish

Directions:

1. Preheat the oven to 450°F and grease a casserole dish with cooking spray.
2. Heat a skillet over medium heat and fry the bacon until crisp. Drain all but 2 tablespoons of the grease.
3. Add the onion to the bacon and continue cooking until the onion is cooked. Spoon the onion and garlic into the fat and set it aside.
4. Turn the heat to high, add the quartered mushrooms to the bacon fat, and brown them over high heat, stirring frequently. Remove the skillet from the heat.
5. Season the sliced potatoes with the salt, pepper, and onion powder and toss to coat the slices evenly. Season the chicken with salt, pepper, and onion powder as well.
6. Layer the ingredients: the chicken, half the bacon and onion mixture, a bit of cheese, mushrooms, bacon mixture, and a little more cheese, and then arrange the potatoes on top.
7. Mix the chicken stock and cream and pour it on top. Cover the baking dish with foil or a lid.
8. Bake for 15 minutes, then reduce the heat to 350°F and bake for another 40 minutes. Remove the foil or the lid and cook for 15 minutes until the top is golden brown and the potatoes are tender.
9. Sprinkle the last of the cheese on top and add the green onion and parsley.

Nutritional Information: Calories: 308, Fat: 12 g, Carbs: 31 g, Protein: 18 g, Sodium: 287 mg

48. Creamy Chicken Quinoa and Broccoli Casserole

Preparation Time: 15 minutes

Cooking Time: 30 minutes

Servings: 4

Ingredients:

- 2 c. chicken broth
- 1 c. milk, divided
- 1 tsp. poultry seasoning
- ½ c. all-purpose flour
- 2 c. water, divided
- 1 c. uncooked quinoa, rinsed
- ¼ c. cooked, crumbled bacon
- 1 lb. boneless skinless chicken breasts
- ¼ c. mozzarella or Monterey jack cheese, shredded
- 3 c. fresh broccoli florets

Directions:

1. Preheat the oven to 400°F and generously grease a 9x13" baking dish
2. Make the sauce. Bring the chicken broth and ½ cup of milk to a low boil in a saucepan. Whisk the other ½ c. milk with the poultry seasoning and flour. Add the mixture to the boiling liquid and whisk until a creamy sauce forms.
3. Mix the sauce with 1 c. water, quinoa, and bacon in a large bowl, and stir to combine. Pour the mixture into the prepared baking dish.
4. Slice the chicken breasts into thin strips and lay them over the quinoa mixture. Bake, uncovered, for 30 minutes.
5. While the casserole is in the oven, place the broccoli in boiling water for 1 minute until it turns bright green, and then run under cold water. Set it aside.
6. Remove the casserole from the oven and check the mixture by stirring it in the pan. If it's not quite cooked, bake for an additional 10–15.
7. When the quinoa and chicken are cooked, and the sauce is thickened, add the broccoli and a little bit of water (up to 1 c.) until the consistency is creamy and smooth, and you can stir it up easily in the pan.
8. Top with the cheese and bake for 5 minutes, or just long enough to melt the cheese.

Nutritional Information: Calories: 363, Fat: 11 g, Carbs: 31 g, Protein: 34 g, Sodium: 467 mg

49. Dreamy Creamy Enchiladas

Preparation Time: 10 minutes

Cooking Time: 10 minutes

Servings: 4

Ingredients:

- 2 c. cooked chicken, shredded
- 1 c. sour cream
- ¼ tsp. salt
- ¼ tsp. black pepper
- 2 tbsps. chives, minced
- ½ c. vegetable oil for frying
- 12 (5-inch) corn tortillas
- 1 (4 oz.) can of chopped green chilies, drained
- 2 c. shredded Monterey Jack cheese

Directions:

1. Preheat the oven to 400°F and grease a 9x13" baking dish with cooking spray. Set out a plate with a paper towel on it to work on.
2. Combine the chicken, sour cream, salt, pepper, and chives in a bowl and set it aside.
3. Heat the oil in a skillet over medium-high heat. Dip the corn tortillas into the hot oil one at a time until softened, about 10 seconds each. Quickly set them on the paper-lined plate and spoon a heaping tablespoon of chicken mixture onto each one. Spread it down the center and roll the tortilla into a cylinder.
4. Place the tortillas seam-side down into the prepared baking dish. When all the tortillas are filled and rolled, sprinkle the green chilies over and top with the shredded Monterey Jack cheese.
5. Bake until the cheese has melted and the enchiladas are hot, 12–15 minutes.

Nutritional Information:

Calories: 434

Fat: 26 g

Carbs: 24 g

Protein: 26 g

Sodium: 540 mg

50. Enchiladas Supreme

Preparation Time: 10 minutes

Cooking Time: 50 minutes

Servings: 4

Ingredients:

- 1 (10.75 oz.) can of condensed cream chicken soup
- 1 ¼ c. sour cream
- ½ tsp. Chili powder
- ½ tsp. cumin
- 1 tbsp. butter
- 1 small onion, chopped
- 1 clove of garlic, minced
- 2 lb. rotisserie chicken, shredded
- 1 (4 oz.) can of chopped green chilies, drained
- 2 tbsps. taco spice mix
- 1 bunch of green onions, chopped and divided
- 1 c. water
- 1 tsp. lemon juice
- 1 tsp. garlic powder
- 5 (12-inch) flour tortillas
- 3 c. cheddar cheese, shredded, divided
- 1 ½ c. enchilada sauce
- ½ c. cilantro, chopped

Directions:

1. Preheat the oven to 350°F. Grease a 9x13" baking dish with cooking spray.
2. Combine the cream of chicken soup, sour cream, chili powder, and cumin in a saucepan. Bring it to a simmer over low heat, stirring occasionally, then turn off the heat and cover the pot.
3. Melt the butter in a skillet over medium heat. Stir in the onion and garlic, and cook until the onion has softened, about 5 minutes.
4. Add the shredded chicken, chopped green chilies, taco seasoning, half of the green onion, and water. Simmer for 10 minutes.
5. Stir in the lemon juice and garlic powder and stir to combine.
6. Mix 1 cup of soup into the skillet with the chicken mixture. Spread the remaining soup mixture into the baking dish.
7. Divide the chicken mixture among the tortillas and sprinkle a generous tablespoon of cheddar over the chicken filling before folding the tortillas. (Half will be left for topping.)
8. Arrange the tortillas seam-side down on the sauce in the prepared baking pan.

9. Pour the enchilada sauce evenly over the enchiladas. Cover with the remaining cheddar cheese. Sprinkle the reserved chopped green onions.
10. Bake until the filling is heated and the cheese is melted and bubbling, about 25 minutes.
11. Garnish with cilantro and serve.

Nutritional Information:

Calories: 709

Fat: 36 g

Carbs: 52 g

Protein: 42 g

Sodium: 1764 mg

51. Healthy Broccoli Chicken Casserole

Preparation Time: 15 minutes

Cooking Time: 20 minutes

Servings: 4

Ingredients:

- 1 lb. raw broccoli, chopped
- 1 lb. cooked shredded chicken, cooked (about 3 large chicken breasts)
- 1 c. brown rice, cooked
- 1 (8 oz.) can of sliced water chestnuts, drained
- ½ c. non-fat Greek yogurt
- ¼ c. milk
- 1 tsp. Garlic salt
- ½ tsp. Black pepper
- ¼ tsp. Thyme
- ¼ tsp. Paprika
- ¼ tsp. rubbed sage
- ½ c. shredded mozzarella
- 1 c. shredded cheddar, divided
- 2 tbsps. panko breadcrumbs

Directions:

1. Preheat the oven to 375°F and prepare a casserole dish with cooking spray.
2. Combine the broccoli, chicken, rice, and water chestnuts in a bowl.
3. Mix Greek yogurt, milk, and seasonings in a separate bowl. Once mixed completely, stir in the mozzarella and half the shredded cheddar.
4. Pour the yogurt mixture over the broccoli and chicken mixture. Mix well.
5. Spoon the casserole into the prepared casserole dish, and cover it with the remaining cheddar and the panko crumbs.
6. Bake for 25 minutes, until the broccoli is cooked through.

Nutritional Information: Calories: 449, Fat: 17 g, Carbs: 33 g, Protein: 46 g, Sodium: 601 mg,

52. King Ranch Chicken and Quinoa Casserole

Preparation Time: 15 minutes

Cooking Time: 40 minutes

Servings: 4

Ingredients:

- 2 c. cooked quinoa
- 1 tbsp. + 2 tsps. olive oil, divided
- 2 c. poblano peppers, chopped (about 3 medium)
- 1 ½ c. onion, chopped
- 1 tbsp. garlic, minced
- 2 tbsps. all-purpose flour
- 2 tsps. ground cumin
- 1 tsp. ancho chili powder
- 2 c. chicken stock
- Salt and pepper to taste
- 1 (14 ½ oz.) can of unsalted fire-roasted tomatoes
- 1 (4 oz.) can of mild chopped green chilies
- 2 c. chicken breast, shredded
- ¾ c. cheddar cheese, shredded, divided
- Cooking spray

Directions:

1. Preheat the oven to 400°F and prepare an 8x8" baking dish with cooking spray.
2. Combine the cooked quinoa and 1 tablespoon of oil in a bowl. Spread the quinoa on a parchment-lined baking sheet and bake for 15 minutes.
3. Meanwhile, heat a large Dutch oven over medium-high heat. Add the remaining 2 teaspoons of oil. Add the poblano pepper, onion, and garlic; sauté 5 minutes.
4. Stir in the flour, cumin, and chili powder, and cook for 1 minute. Add the stock, salt and pepper, tomatoes, and chopped green chilies. Bring it to a boil, reduce the heat, and simmer for 5 minutes.
5. Remove the pan from the heat and stir in the chicken.
6. Pour half of the chicken mixture into the baking dish, and top with half of the quinoa and a quarter of the cheese.
7. Repeat the layers once with the remaining chicken mixture, remaining quinoa, and the rest of the cheese. Bake for 25 minutes.

Nutritional Information: Calories: 462, Fat: 19 g, Carbs: 45 g, Protein: 32 g, Sodium: 689 mg

53. Tex-Mex Casserole

Preparation Time: 15 minutes

Cooking Time: 40 minutes

Servings: 4

Ingredients:

- 2 tbsps. vegetable oil
- 2 c. cooked chicken breasts, shredded meat
- 1 tbsp. taco spice mix
- 1 (15 oz.) can of black beans, rinsed and drained
- 1 (8 ¾ oz.) can of sweet corn, drained
- 1 c. white rice, cooked
- ¼ c. salsa
- Water as needed
- 1 c. shredded Mexican-style cheese
- 1 ½ c. crushed plain tortilla chips
- ½ c. cilantro, chopped

Directions:

1. Preheat the oven to 350°F and prepare a 9x13 baking pan with cooking spray.
2. Place a large skillet over medium-high heat and heat the oil. Sauté the chicken until it is cooked through.
3. Add the taco seasoning, beans, corn, rice, salsa, and a little water to prevent it from drying. Cover the skillet and simmer over medium-low heat for 10 minutes.
4. Transfer the chicken mixture to the baking dish. Top with half the cheese and all the crushed tortilla chips.
5. Bake for 15 minutes. Add the remaining cheese and bake until it is melted and bubbly. Garnish with cilantro before serving.

Nutritional Information:

Calories: 531

Fat: 21 g

Carbs: 53 g

Protein: 36 g

Sodium: 1430 mg

54. Turkey Sausage Potato Bake

Preparation Time: 20 minutes

Cooking Time: 40 minutes

Servings: 4

Ingredients:

- 2 (4 oz.) hot turkey Italian sausage links, casings removed
- 1 tbsp. butter
- 2 c. onion, chopped
- 4 oz. white mushrooms, sliced
- 2 lb. red potatoes, coarsely chopped
- 1 tsp. salt
- 1 tsp. Pepper
- ½ tsp. Thyme
- ¼ tsp. paprika
- ½ c. chicken broth
- ½ c. Swiss cheese, shredded
- ½ c. Parmesan cheese, shredded
- ¼ c. fresh parsley, chopped

Directions:

1. Preheat the oven to 400°F, and spray a 3-quart baking dish with cooking spray
2. Heat a large, non-stick skillet over medium-high heat. Add the sausage, and sauté for 5 minutes or until browned, stirring to crumble.
3. Remove the sausage to a plate and drain it on a paper towel.
4. Melt the butter in the pan. Add the onion and cook for 4 minutes, stirring occasionally. Add the mushrooms and sauté for 6 minutes, stirring occasionally.
5. Add the potatoes, salt, pepper, thyme, and paprika. Cook until browned, about 5 minutes.
6. Stir in the sausage and broth.
7. Spoon the potato mixture into the prepared baking dish, and top with cheese.
8. Cover, and bake for 30 minutes. Uncover, and bake for an additional 15 minutes or until golden. Sprinkle with fresh parsley and serve.

Nutritional Information: Calories: 358, Fat: 13 g, Carbs: 40 g, Protein: 19 g, Sodium: 619 mg

55. Turkey Taco Mexican Lasagna

Preparation Time: 15 minutes

Cooking Time: 30 minutes

Servings: 4

Ingredients:

- 1 tbsp. olive oil
- 1 c. bell pepper, chopped
- 1 jalapeño pepper finely diced
- 1 c. sweet onion, chopped
- 2 cloves garlic, crushed and minced
- 1 ½ lbs. leftover turkey meat
- 1 (15 oz.) can of crushed tomatoes

For the Taco Spice Mix:

- 1 ½ tbsp. cumin
- 1 ½ tsps. paprika
- 1 ½ tsps. salt
- 1 tsp. chili powder
- 1 tsp. Cornstarch
- ½ tsp. Garlic powder
- ½ tsp. Black pepper
- ½ tsp. Red pepper flakes
- ¼ tsp. cayenne pepper
- 1 c. frozen corn kernels
- 1 (15 oz.) can of black beans, drained
- 2 c. shredded cheese (cheddar or Monterey Jack)
- 12 corn tortillas
- Sour cream
- ½ c. green onions, chopped

Directions:

1. Preheat the oven to 350°F and prepare a 9x13" baking dish with cooking spray.
2. Heat the oil in a large skillet over medium heat. Add the bell pepper, jalapeño, and onion. Sauté for 5 minutes.
3. Add the garlic and the cooked turkey to the skillet, and cook for 3–4 minutes, until the garlic is aromatic and the turkey is warmed through.
4. Add the crushed tomatoes and simmer for a few minutes.

5. Combine the spice ingredients in a small bowl. Sprinkle the mixture into the skillet, stir, and let it simmer for another 5 minutes.
6. Start layering the Mexican lasagna with one-third of the turkey-tomato mixture.
7. Arrange 6 tortillas on that (cutting them if necessary), and cover with another third of the turkey mixture, half the corn, half the beans, and 1 cup of shredded cheese.
8. Repeat with the remaining tortillas, turkey, corn, beans, and cheese. Place aluminum foil over the baking dish and bake for 30 minutes.
9. Remove the aluminum foil and continue baking for 5 more minutes.
10. Let it sit for at least 10 minutes before serving. You can serve it with a dollop of sour cream and some green onion on top if you like.

Nutritional Information:

Calories: 307

Fat: 13 g

Carbs: 25 g

Protein: 23 g

Sodium: 777 mg

56. Zucchini Chicken Bake

Preparation Time: 20 minutes

Cooking Time: 30 minutes

Servings: 4

Ingredients:

- 1 egg
- 1 tbsp. water
- Salt and pepper to taste
- 1 c. dry bread crumbs, divided
- 4 tbsps. olive oil, divided
- 4 skinless, boneless chicken breast halves
- 5 zucchinis, sliced
- 1 small onion, minced
- 3 cloves garlic, minced
- 4 tomatoes, sliced
- 1 c. mozzarella cheese, shredded, divided
- 2 tsps. Fresh basil, chopped

Directions:

1. Preheat the oven to 400°F. Lightly grease a 9x13" baking dish.
2. Beat the egg, water, salt, and pepper in a shallow bowl. Set 2 tablespoons of bread crumbs aside and pour the remaining bread crumbs into a large resealable plastic bag.
3. Dip the chicken pieces in the egg mixture, place them in the bag and shake to coat.
4. Heat 2 tablespoons of olive oil in a large skillet over medium. Cook the chicken until browned, 2 to 3 minutes per side. Remove the chicken from the pan.
5. Add the remaining 2 tablespoons of oil to the skillet. Add the zucchini, onion, and garlic, and cook over medium heat until the zucchini is slightly tender and the onion is softened, about 2 minutes. Transfer the vegetables to the prepared baking dish.
6. Sprinkle the reserved bread crumbs over the zucchini. Top with tomato slices, three-quarters of the mozzarella cheese, and basil. Place the chicken on top.
7. Cover with aluminum foil and bake until the chicken is no longer pink in the center, about 25 minutes.
8. Uncover, and sprinkle with the remaining mozzarella cheese. Bake until the cheese is melted, about 5 minutes.

Nutritional Information: Calories: 506, Fat: 24 g, Carbs: 34 g, Protein: 40 g, Sodium: 768 mg

57. Easy Tex-Mex Chicken

Preparation Time: 20 minutes

Cooking Time: 20 minutes

Servings: 4

Ingredients:

- 4 boneless, skinless chicken breasts
- 1 tbsp. olive oil
- 1 clove of garlic, minced
- Salt and pepper to taste
- ½ tsp. ground cumin
- ½ tsp. chili powder
- Pinch red pepper flakes
- 1 c. salsa
- 1 c. shredded cheddar cheese
- Cooked white rice for serving

Directions:

1. Preheat the oven to 375°F and grease an 8x8" baking pan with cooking spray.
2. Heat a skillet over medium heat and warm the oil. Rub the chicken pieces with garlic, salt, pepper, cumin, chili powder, and red pepper flakes.
3. Cook the chicken until it is brown on both sides and no longer pink in the middle, about 10 minutes.
4. Place the chicken in the baking dish. Top with salsa and cheese and bake until the cheese is bubbly and starts to brown, about 20 minutes.
5. Serve with rice, if desired.

Nutritional Information:

Calories: 286

Fat: 15 g

Carbs: 5 g

Protein: 35 g

Sodium: 641 mg

58. Southern Chicken and Biscuit Bake

Preparation Time: 20 minutes

Cooking Time: 50 minutes

Servings: 4

Ingredients:

- ¼ c. butter
- 2 cloves garlic, minced
- 1 small onion, chopped
- 2 stalks of celery, chopped
- ¼ c. baby carrots, chopped
- ½ c. all-purpose flour
- 1 tsp. white sugar
- 1 tsp. salt
- 1 tsp. dried marjoram
- ½ tsp. ground black pepper
- 4 c. chicken broth
- 1 c. frozen peas, thawed
- 4 c. diced, cooked chicken meat
- 2 c. buttermilk baking mix
- 2 tsps. dried basil
- ⅔ c. milk

Directions:

1. Preheat the oven to 350°F and coat a 9x13" baking dish with cooking spray.
2. In a skillet, melt the butter over medium-high heat. Cook and stir in the garlic, onion, celery, and carrots until they are tender. Mix in the flour, sugar, salt, marjoram, and pepper.
3. Stir in the broth and bring the mixture to a boil. Stirring constantly, boil for 1 minute. Reduce the heat and stir in the peas and the chicken. Simmer for 5 minutes, then transfer the mixture to the prepared baking dish.
4. In a medium bowl, combine the baking mix and basil. Stir in the milk to form a dough. Divide the dough into 8 balls. On floured wax paper, use your hand's palm to flatten each dough ball into a circular shape and place them on top of the chicken mixture.
5. Bake for 30 minutes. Cover with foil and bake for 10 more minutes. To serve, spoon the chicken mixture over the biscuits.

Nutritional Information: Calories: 450, Fat: 13 g, Carbs: 48 g, Protein: 33 g, Sodium: 205 mg

59. Beef Quick Pastitsio

Preparation Time: 20 minutes

Cooking Time: 40 minutes

Servings: 4

Ingredients:

- 8 oz. uncooked penne
- 1 tbsp. olive oil
- 1 lb. ground beef
- 1 large onion, diced
- 5 cloves garlic, minced
- 1 tsp. Salt
- ½ tsp. Black pepper
- ¼ tsp. dried oregano
- 1 tbsp. all-purpose flour
- 2 c. milk
- 1 (14 ½ oz.) can of diced tomatoes, drained
- 8 oz. reduced fat cream cheese
- ½ c. mozzarella cheese, shredded
- 2 tbsps. Chopped fresh flat-leaf parsley

Directions:

1. Preheat the broiler and coat a 9x13" baking pan with cooking spray.
2. Cook the pasta according to the package directions. Drain well.
3. Meanwhile, heat a large skillet over medium-high heat. Warm the olive oil and add the beef to the pan. Sauté for 5 minutes or until browned, stirring to crumble. Drain any excess grease.
4. Add the onion and sauté until tender, stirring occasionally. Add the garlic and cook for 1 more minute, stirring constantly.
5. Season the mixture with salt, pepper, and oregano. Sprinkle the flour over the meat and cook for 1 minute, stirring frequently.
6. Stir in the milk, tomatoes, and cream cheese until smooth. Bring the mixture to a simmer. Cook until it is heated through, and stir in the pasta.
7. Spoon the pasta mixture into the baking dish and sprinkle it with the mozzarella.
8. Broil for 4 minutes or until golden. Sprinkle with parsley.

Nutritional Information: Calories: 431, Fat: 16 g, Carbs: 42 g, Protein: 28 g, Sodium: 679 mg

60. Unstuffed Cabbage Casserole

Preparation Time: 20 minutes

Cooking Time: 70 minutes

Servings: 4

Ingredients:

- 2 lb. cabbage, roughly chopped
- 1 lb. ground beef
- 2 tbsps. butter
- 1 large onion, chopped
- 4 cloves garlic, minced
- ½ c. tomato paste
- ½ c. tomatoes, diced
- 1 c. rice, rinsed
- 1 ½ tsps. salt
- 1 tsp. black pepper
- 1 tsp. Italian seasoning
- 1 bunch of parsley, chopped
- ¾ c. water
- 2 cans of condensed tomato soup

Directions:

1. Blanch the cabbage in boiling water for 5–10 minutes until tender. Drain, cover, and set aside.
2. Meanwhile, cook the ground beef over medium heat, and drain any excess fat.
3. Push the beef to the side, and add the butter, onion, and garlic. Stir in the vegetables and cook for 5–10 minutes, covered.
4. Add the tomato paste, chopped tomatoes, rice, salt, pepper, Italian seasoning, parsley, and water. Stir well.
5. Cover, and cook on medium-low until the water is absorbed and the rice is cooked, about 15 minutes.
6. Preheat the oven to 350°F and coat a 3-quart casserole dish with cooking spray.
7. Stir in the cabbage and spoon the mixture into the baking dish. Spread the condensed tomato soup on top.
8. Bake for 30 minutes.

Nutritional Information: Calories: 466, Fat: 21 g, Carbs: 52 g, Protein: 20 g, Sodium: 1130 mg

61. Superfood Taco Casserole

Preparation Time: 20 minutes

Cooking Time: 40 minutes

Servings: 4

Ingredients:

- 1 tbsp. vegetable oil
- 1 lb. ground beef
- 1 c. chicken stock
- 1 c. uncooked quinoa, rinsed
- 1 (28 oz.) can of diced tomatoes
- 2 tbsps. taco spice mix
- 1 red bell pepper, chopped
- 3 green onions (white and greens only), chopped
- 1 c. corn kernels
- 1 c. canned black beans, rinsed and drained
- 3 c. kale, chopped and stemmed
- 1 c. cheddar or Monterey Jack cheese, shredded

Directions:

1. Preheat the oven to 350°F and coat a 9x13" baking dish with cooking spray.
2. Heat the vegetable oil in a skillet and cook the ground beef. Drain any excess grease.
3. Pour the chicken stock into the baking dish and stir in the dry quinoa.
4. In a large bowl, combine the tomatoes with the spices, and pour half of this mixture over the quinoa.
5. Top with ground beef, bell pepper, green onions, corn, black beans, and kale.
6. Pour the remaining tomatoes on top, and sprinkle with cheese.
7. Cover the dish with foil, bake for 45 minutes, then remove the foil and continue baking for 15 minutes.

Nutritional Information:

Calories: 448

Fat: 21 g

Carbs: 47 g

Protein: 28 g

Sodium: 769 mg

62. Beefy Tots Casserole

Preparation Time: 20 minutes

Cooking Time: 50 minutes

Servings: 4

Ingredients:

- 1 (32 oz.) bag of frozen bite-size potato nuggets (such as Tater Tots®) divided
- 1 lb. ground beef
- 1 large onion, chopped
- 1 tbsp. Worcestershire sauce
- 1 tsp. Montreal-style steak seasoning
- 1 tsp. garlic powder
- 1 (10 ¾ oz.) can condense cream of mushroom soup
- ½ c. milk
- 1 ½ c. cheddar cheese, shredded, divided
- ½ c. cilantro for garnishing

Directions:

1. Preheat the oven to 350°F and coat a 9x13" casserole dish with cooking spray.
2. Spread 20 potato nuggets in the casserole dish, and bake until warmed through, about 10 minutes.
3. Meanwhile, heat a large skillet over medium-high heat. Cook and stir the beef and onion until the beef is completely browned, 5–7 minutes. Drain any excess grease.
4. Season the beef mixture with the Worcestershire sauce, steak seasoning, and garlic powder.
5. Combine the cream of mushroom soup, milk, ½ cup of Cheddar cheese, and 1 teaspoon of Worcestershire sauce in a bowl.
6. Using a fork or potato masher, crush the warmed potato nuggets in the casserole dish to cover the bottom completely. Spread the ground beef mixture over the mashed potato nuggets. Pour the soup mixture evenly over the beef layer. Top with remaining potato nuggets and sprinkle the remaining cheddar cheese evenly over the top.
7. Bake until the casserole is bubbly and the potatoes are golden brown, 30–40 minutes. Sprinkle with cilantro and serve.

Nutritional Information: Calories: 477, Fat: 27 g, Carbs: 38 g, Protein: 25 g, Sodium: 1219 mg

63. Beef Goulash

Preparation Time: 20 minutes

Cooking Time: 60 minutes

Servings: 4

Ingredients:

- 3 tbsps. butter, divided
- 2 lb. beef chuck, cut into chunks
- 2 tbsps. all-purpose flour
- 1 large onion, thinly sliced
- 2 cloves garlic, minced
- ½ green pepper, deseeded and thinly sliced
- ½ red pepper, deseeded and thinly sliced
- 2 tbsps. tomato paste
- 2 tbsps. paprika (good quality is essential)
- 1 ½ c. canned tomatoes, drained
- ⅓ c. dry white wine
- 1 ½ c. beef stock
- Salt and pepper to taste
- ⅔ c. sour cream
- 2 tbsps. parsley, chopped
- Mashed potatoes for serving

Directions:

1. Preheat the oven to 350°F.
2. Heat 2 tablespoons of butter in a Dutch oven. Sprinkle the beef with the flour and brown it well, working in batches. Set the browned meat aside.
3. Add the remaining butter to the pot, and cook the onion, garlic, green pepper, and red pepper until they are softened, about 5 minutes.
4. Return the beef to the pot and stir in the tomato paste and paprika. Cook, stirring, for 2 minutes.
5. Add the tomatoes, white wine, and beef stock. Cover and bake for 1 ½ – 2 hours, until the meat is tender.
6. Season with salt and freshly ground pepper.
7. Stir in the sour cream and garnish with parsley. Serve with potatoes, if desired.

Nutritional Information: Calories: 386, Fat: 15 g, Carbs: 34 g, Protein: 28 g, Sodium: 1466 mg

64. Beef Stew Bake

Preparation Time: 20 minutes

Cooking Time: 2 hours 40 minutes

Servings: 4

Ingredients:

- 3 c. water
- 1 tbsp. vegetable oil
- 1 tbsp. butter
- 2 celery ribs, roughly chopped
- 1 large onion, roughly chopped
- 3 large carrots, roughly chopped
- 2 small potatoes, peeled and chopped
- 3 cloves garlic, roughly chopped
- 3 bay leaves
- 3 sprigs of thyme divided
- 2 tbsps. all-purpose flour
- 2 tbsps. tomato purée
- 2 tbsps. Worcestershire sauce
- 2 beef stock cubes, crumbled
- 2 lb. stewing beef in large chunks

Directions:

1. Heat the oven to 350°F, and boil 3 cups of water.
2. In a Dutch oven, warm the vegetable oil and butter together. Cook the celery, onion, carrots, potatoes, garlic, bay leaves, and 1 thyme sprig. Cook for 10 minutes, stirring occasionally.
3. Stir in the flour, followed by the tomato purée, Worcestershire sauce, beef stock cubes, and the remaining thyme sprigs.
4. Gradually stir in hot water, add the beef and bring the mixture to a gentle simmer.
5. Cover and bake for 2 ½ hours, then uncover and cook for ½ to 1 hour more, until the meat is tender and the sauce is thickened.
6. Remove the thyme twigs and bay leaves before serving.

Nutritional Information: Calories: 538, Fat: 33 g, Carbs: 16 g, Protein: 36 g, Sodium: 1600 mg

65. Easy Beef Casserole

Preparation Time: 20 minutes

Cooking Time: 40 minutes

Servings: 4

Ingredients:

- 3 ½ c. farfalle (bow tie) pasta, uncooked
- 1 lb. ground beef
- 2 cloves garlic, minced
- 1 (15 oz.) can of tomato sauce
- 1 c. sour cream
- 1 tsp. dried thyme
- ½ c. green olives, chopped
- ½ c. parsley, chopped
- 1 c. shredded mozzarella cheese

Directions:

1. Preheat the oven to 350°F and prepare a 2-quart casserole dish with cooking spray.
2. Bring a pot of water to a boil. Add the pasta, and cook until tender, about 8 minutes.
3. Crumble the ground beef into a skillet and cook over medium-high heat. Drain any excess grease, and stir in the garlic, tomato sauce, sour cream, and thyme.
4. Place the cooked pasta in the casserole dish and spoon the ground beef mixture over it. Sprinkle on the olives and the parsley
5. Top with shredded cheese, and bake for 30 minutes, until heated and lightly browned on the top.

Nutritional Information:

Calories: 386

Fat: 22 g

Carbs: 24 g

Protein: 24 g

Sodium: 704 mg

66. Ravioli Twist

Preparation Time: 20 minutes

Cooking Time: 40 minutes

Servings: 4

Ingredients:

- 16 oz. dry pasta
- 1 (10 oz.) package of frozen, chopped spinach
- 1 lb. lean ground beef
- 1 small chopped onion, diced
- 1 clove of garlic, minced
- 1 (8 oz.) can of tomato sauce
- 1 (6 oz.) can of tomato paste
- 2 c. pasta sauce
- ½ c. bread crumbs
- 2 eggs, beaten
- ¼ c. chicken or beef broth
- 1 c. mozzarella cheese, shredded

Directions:

1. Preheat the oven to 350°F and prepare a 9x13" baking dish with cooking spray.
2. In a medium pot, cook the pasta in boiling salted water until al dente. Drain well.
3. Cook the spinach according to the package directions.
4. Meanwhile, brown the ground beef in a large skillet over medium heat, and drain the fat. Add the chopped onion and minced garlic. Stir in the tomato sauce, tomato paste, and pasta sauce. Simmer for 10 minutes.
5. Combine the cooked spinach, pasta, bread crumbs, eggs, broth or water, and shredded cheese.
6. Spread the spinach mixture evenly in the baking dish. Top with the meat mixture. Cover with aluminum foil.
7. Bake for 30 minutes and serve.

Nutritional Information:

Calories: 526

Fat: 25 g

Carbs: 52 g

Protein: 26 g

Sodium: 779 mg

67. Spaghetti Squash Beef and Bubble

Preparation Time: 20 minutes

Cooking Time: 60 minutes

Servings: 4

Ingredients:

- 1 spaghetti squash, halved and seeded
- 1 lb. ground beef
- ½ c. diced green bell pepper
- ½ c. diced red bell pepper
- ¼ c. diced red onion
- 2 cloves garlic, minced
- 1 (14 ½ oz.) can of Italian-style diced tomatoes, drained
- ½ c. prepared salsa
- 1 ½ tsps. Italian seasoning
- Salt and pepper to taste
- 2 ¼ c. cheddar cheese, shredded, divided

Directions:

1. Preheat the oven to 375°F.
2. Place the squash on a baking sheet, and bake it for 40 minutes or until tender. Remove it from the heat, cool it, and shred the pulp with a fork.
3. Reduce the oven temperature to 350°F. Lightly grease a casserole dish.
4. In a skillet over medium heat, cook the ground beef. Drain any excess grease, and mix in green, red onion, and garlic. Continue to cook and stir until the vegetables are tender.
5. Mix the shredded squash, tomatoes, and salsa into the skillet and season with Italian seasoning, salt, and pepper. Cook and stir until heated through.
6. Remove the skillet from the heat, and mix in 2 cups of cheese until melted. Transfer to the prepared casserole dish.
7. Bake for 25 minutes, then sprinkle with the remaining cheese and continue baking for 5 minutes until the cheese is melted.

Nutritional Information: Calories: 399, Fat: 26 g, Carbs: 13 g, Protein: 27 g, Sodium: 590 mg

68. Squash Pasta

Preparation Time: 20 minutes

Cooking Time: 40 minutes

Servings: 4

Ingredients:

- 1 tsp. salt, divided
- ½ tsp. dried rosemary
- Salt and pepper to taste
- 3 c. butternut squash, peeled and cut into 1-inch cubes
- ½ lb. hickory-smoked bacon slices (uncooked)
- ½ c. shallots, thinly sliced
- 8 oz. small penne or macaroni pasta (uncooked)
- ¼ c. all-purpose flour
- 2 c. milk
- ¾ c. sharp provolone cheese, shredded
- ⅓ c. fresh Parmesan cheese, grated

Directions:

1. Spray cooking spray in a 2-quart baking dish and preheat the oven to 425°F.
2. Rosemary and pepper should be combined with ¼ teaspoon of salt. Squash should be placed on a foil-lined baking pan with cooking spray. Sprinkle the salt mixture over it.
3. Bake for 45 minutes or until soft and just beginning to color. Turn up the oven's heat to 450°F.
4. In the meantime, in a big nonstick skillet, fry the bacon until crisp. Remove the bacon from the pan by reserving 1 tablespoon of the bacon oil. Set the bacon aside after crumbling it.
5. Medium-high heat is increased. The shallots should be added to the pan and cooked for a few minutes until soft. Set aside after combining the bacon, shallots, and squash mixture.
6. Follow the instructions on the pasta package for cooking.
7. Mix the flour and the remaining salt in a Dutch oven over medium-high heat. Bring it to a boil while whisking continuously while you add the milk in stages. Remove it from the fire after cooking for 1 minute or when it slightly thickens.
8. When the provolone has melted, add it and continue stirring. The cheese sauce should be combined with the pasta.
9. The squash mixture should be placed on top of the pasta mixture in the baking dish. Parmesan cheese should be distributed equally.
10. The cheese should melt and start to color after 10 minutes of baking.

Nutritional Information: Calories: 494, Fat: 21 g, Carbs: 56 g, Protein: 21 g, Sodium: 1006 mg

69. Broccoli Sausage Quinoa Casserole

Preparation Time: 20 minutes

Cooking Time: 40 minutes

Servings: 4

Ingredients:

- 2 ½ c. water
- 2 c. uncooked quinoa, rinsed and drained
- ¼ c. butter, divided
- 1 small onion, diced
- ½ c. carrot, peeled and diced
- 4 (4 oz.) links of sweet chicken Italian sausage, casings removed
- ¼ c. all-purpose flour
- 3 cloves garlic, minced
- 2 c. whole milk
- 2 c. unsalted chicken stock
- 6 c. fresh broccoli florets, chopped
- 1 tbsp. fresh thyme divided
- Salt and pepper to taste
- ¼ tsp. crushed red pepper
- ½ c. whole wheat breadcrumbs
- 1 c. cheddar cheese, shredded

Directions:

1. Preheat the oven to 400°F and prepare two 8x8" baking pans with cooking spray.
2. Boil the water in a medium saucepan and add the quinoa. Reduce the heat, cover, and simmer for 12–14 minutes or until the liquid is absorbed. Remove the pot from the heat and let it stand for 5 minutes.
3. Heat a large Dutch oven over medium-high heat. Add 1 tablespoon of butter and swirl until it's melted.
4. Add the onion, carrot, and sausage. Cook for 7 minutes, stirring to crumble the sausage. Remove the sausage mixture to a bowl, and cover.
5. Add flour, remaining butter, and garlic to the drippings in the pan and cook for 2 minutes, stirring frequently. Add the milk and stock and bring it to a boil.
6. Cook for 2 minutes, whisking constantly. Reduce the heat to medium. Stir in the broccoli, 2 teaspoons of thyme, salt, black pepper, and red pepper flakes—cover and cook for 2 minutes.
7. Stir in the quinoa and the sausage mixture.
8. Divide the quinoa mixture between the baking dishes.
9. In a mixing bowl, combine the panko with the remaining teaspoon of thyme and season with salt and pepper. Stir in the cheddar and divide the mixture over the two pans.
10. Bake for 20 minutes or until browned.

Nutritional Information:

Calories: 296

Fat: 13 g

Carbs: 28 g

Protein: 17 g

Sodium: 399 mg

70. Creamy Cauliflower with Bacon

Preparation Time: 20 minutes

Cooking Time: 30 minutes

Servings: 4

Ingredients:

- 1 large head of cauliflower
- 4–6 strips of bacon
- 1 c. sour cream
- ½ c. shredded Monterey jack cheese, divided
- Salt and pepper to taste

Directions:

1. Preheat the oven to 350°F, and lightly grease a casserole dish with olive oil spray.
2. Fill a large pot with 1–2" of water and bring it to a boil. Cut the cauliflower into bite-sized pieces and add it to the boiling water, cover it, and reduce the heat to low.
3. Steam the cauliflower until it is fork-tender and drains well.
4. Meanwhile, cook the bacon until crisp. Remove the bacon and crumble, reserving the bacon grease.
5. Pour the cauliflower into the casserole dish and drizzle the bacon grease on top. Stir in the sour cream, half the shredded cheese, and half the crumbled bacon. Stir until well-coated.
6. Top with the remaining cheese and bacon, and bake for 15–20 minutes or until the cheese is melted.

Nutritional Information:

Calories: 213

Fat: 14 g

Carbs: 10 g

Protein: 11 g

Sodium: 558 mg

71. Quick Shepherd's Pie

Preparation Time: 10 minutes

Cooking Time: 40 minutes

Servings: 4

Ingredients:

- 1 (24 oz.) bag of frozen mashed potatoes
- ½ c. milk
- 3 tbsps. Butter, divided
- ¾ tsp. salt, divided
- 12 oz. pork loin, cut into ½-inch pieces
- ½ tsp. freshly ground black pepper
- 1 medium onion, diced
- 1 (6 oz.) microwavable bag of peeled baby carrots
- 1 tbsp. tomato paste
- ⅓ c. dry red wine
- 2 tbsps. all-purpose flour
- 2 c. beef broth
- 1 c. frozen green peas
- 1 tbsp. Summer savory
- ½ tsp. Marjoram
- ½ tsp. Rosemary

Directions:

1. The broiler should be set at high. Follow the instructions on the potato's package for microwave cooking. ¼ teaspoon salt, 2 tablespoons of butter, and milk should all be stirred.
2. When the potatoes are cooking, heat a Dutch oven on medium-high. Swirl in the remaining butter to coat the pan. Sprinkle the remaining salt and pepper evenly over the pork.
3. After browning the pork on all sides for 6 minutes, take it from the pan.
4. Stirring sporadically during the 4 minutes of sautéing the onion
5. Cook the carrots in the microwave on HIGH for 1 ½ minutes while the onion cooks.
6. Slice the carrots into 1-inch pieces after removing them from the bag.
7. As you constantly stir, sauté the onions and tomato paste together for 1 minute. Use the wine to clean the pot.
8. Stir continuously for a minute after adding the flour. Stir continuously, and add the broth gradually.
9. Add the herbs, peas, and carrot slices after stirring. It should be brought to a boil and then cooked for 4 minutes, stirring occasionally or until somewhat thick. Stir in the browned meat after turning the heat off.
10. Place the mashed potato mixture on top of it and spoon it into a 2-quart ceramic casserole dish that can be broiler-safe. 4 minutes under the broiler or until the top is barely browned.

Nutritional Information:

Calories: 377

Fat: 14 g

Carbs: 40 g

Protein: 20 g

Sodium: 536 mg

72. Pork and Cabbage

Preparation Time: 30 minutes

Cooking Time: 40 minutes

Servings: 4

Ingredients:

- 4 slices of bacon
- 6 country-style pork ribs
- Salt and pepper to taste
- 5 c. cabbage, shredded
- 1 medium onion, chopped
- 1 large apple, chopped
- 3 carrots, julienned
- ¾ c. apple cider (or juice)
- 1 tsp. celery seed

Directions:

1. Preheat the oven to 350°F and grease a 9x13" casserole dish.
2. In a medium skillet, cook the bacon. Remove it from the drippings and crumble it in a bowl.
3. Season the ribs with salt and pepper and cook them in the bacon grease for 3-4 minutes on high heat, turning once. Remove them to the casserole dish.
4. Cook the cabbage and onion until softened in the bacon grease.
5. Mix in the apple, carrots, apple cider, and celery seed. Spoon this mixture over top of the pork, and sprinkle with bacon.
6. Cover with foil and bake for 30–45 minutes.

Nutritional Information:

Calories: 322

Fat: 18 g

Carbs: 13 g

Protein: 27 g

Sodium: 349.7 mg

73. Succotash with Crunchy Bacon Topping

Preparation Time: 20 minutes

Cooking Time: 40 minutes

Servings: 4

Ingredients:

- 2 c. frozen baby lima beans
- 6 slices bacon
- 1 small onion, diced
- ½ red bell pepper, diced
- ½ tsp. salt, divided
- 2 cloves garlic, minced
- 2 c. frozen corn kernels, thawed
- 3 tbsps. all-purpose flour
- 1 ⅓ c. milk, divided
- ¼ tsp. black pepper
- ¾ c. sharp cheddar cheese, shredded
- 15 round buttery crackers, coarsely crushed

Directions:

1. Cooking spray should be used to coat an 8x8" casserole dish before preheating the oven to 375°F.
2. Lima beans should be crisp-tender after 5 minutes of boiling water; drain.
3. In a sizable nonstick skillet set over medium heat, cook the bacon until crisp. It should be taken out of the pan while leaving 2 teaspoons of drippings. Bacon should be crumbled and placed aside.
4. Add the onion, bell pepper, ¼ teaspoon of salt, and garlic to the pan drippings. Cook for 4 minutes, stirring regularly, or until tender. Corn and lima beans are now added.
5. Mix the flour and ⅓ cup milk in a small bowl to create a slurry.
6. The remaining milk, black pepper, and slurry should all be added to the corn mixture. Cook for 3 minutes over medium heat or until thick and bubbling. Take it off the heat.
7. After adding, whisk in the cheese until it melts. Fill the baking dish with the mixture.
8. On top of the dish, sprinkle the bacon and cracker crumbs. Bake for 20 minutes or until the edges are bubbling and the top is lightly browned.

Nutritional Information: Calories: 258, Fat: 8 g, Carbs: 34 g, Protein: 13 g, Sodium: 514 mg

74. Sausage and Caramelized Onion Bread Pudding

Preparation Time: 20 minutes

Cooking Time: 60 minutes

Servings: 4

Ingredients:

- 1 ⅓ c. milk
- ¼ tsp. Dry mustard
- ⅛ tsp. salt
- 2 large eggs
- 1 large egg white
- 8 slices of day-old French bread, cut into 1-inch cubes
- 2 tbsps. unsalted butter
- 2 large yellow onions, diced
- 1 tsp. rubbed sage
- Salt and pepper to taste
- ¼ c. apple juice
- 4 oz. Italian sausage, casings removed
- ¾ c. sharp cheddar cheese, shredded, divided

Directions:

1. Whisk together the milk, mustard, salt, eggs, and egg whites in a big bowl. Bread cubes should be added and carefully coated. Give the bread mixture 20 minutes to stand.
2. Preheat the oven to 350°F.
3. A sizable nonstick skillet should be heated to medium. Spray some cooking spray on the pan. The onions should be cooked for 10 minutes with sporadic stirring. Cook for 5 more minutes while occasionally stirring after adding the juice. Add sage, salt, and pepper to taste.
4. In the interim, crumble the sausage into a different pan. Cook for 10 minutes, stirring regularly, or until browned. After draining the grease and turning off the heat, give it 5 minutes to stand.
5. Stir carefully to combine the bread mixture with the sausage and onions thoroughly. The cheese is folded in.
6. Bake for 40 minutes, or until firm and lightly browned, after spooning the mixture into the baking dish. 10 minutes should pass before serving.

Nutritional Information: Calories: 481, Fat: 22 g, Carbs: 46 g, Protein: 27 g, Sodium: 897 mg

75. Bacon, Gruyère, and Ham Strata

Preparation Time: 20 minutes

Cooking Time: 40 minutes

Servings: 4

Ingredients:

- 2 c. milk
- 1 c. scallions, chopped
- 4 eggs, lightly beaten
- 1 tbsp. Dijon mustard
- ¼ tsp. cayenne pepper
- 10 c. sourdough bread, cut into ½-inch cubes toasted
- ¼ c. ham, diced
- 1 c. Gruyère cheese, shredded
- 4 bacon slices, cooked and crumbled

Directions:

1. Combine the milk, scallions, eggs, mustard, and pepper in a large bowl, stirring with a whisk. Add the bread cubes and ham; stir well to combine.
2. Spray a 2-quart baking pan with cooking spray. Pour the mixture in, and sprinkle with shredded cheese—cover and chill for 8 hours or overnight.
3. Preheat the oven to 350°F.
4. Uncover the dish and bake for 20 minutes. Sprinkle with bacon. Bake another 15 minutes or until the bread mixture is set and the cheese is melted.

Nutritional Information:

Calories: 355

Fat: 14 g

Carbs: 3 g

Protein: 22 g

Sodium: 849 mg

76. Pesto Chicken Casserole

Preparation Time: 20 minutes

Cooking Time: 40 minutes

Servings: 4

Ingredients:

- 1 ½ lbs. chicken thighs or chicken breasts
- 2 oz. butter for frying
- 3 oz. red pesto or green pesto
- 1½ c. heavy whipping cream
- 8 tbsps. pitted olives
- 8 oz. feta cheese, diced
- 1 garlic clove, finely chopped
- Salt and pepper

For Serving:

- 5 1/3 oz. leafy greens
- 4 tbsps. olive oil
- Sea salt and ground black pepper

Directions:

1. Set the oven's temperature to 400°F (200°C).
2. Chicken breasts or thighs should be cut into bite-sized pieces. Add salt and pepper to taste.
3. Chicken pieces should be fried in batches in a big skillet with butter over medium-high heat until golden brown.
4. In a bowl, combine pesto and heavy cream.
5. Put the fried chicken pieces, feta cheese, garlic, and olives in a baking dish. Put the pesto in.
6. Bake for 20 to 30 minutes or until the dish bubbles and the edges are lightly browned.

Nutritional Information:

Calories: 49

Fat: 1.9 g

Carbohydrates: 7 g

Protein: 3 g

77. Thai Fish Coconut Curry Casserole

Preparation Time: 20 minutes

Cooking Time: 40 minutes

Servings: 4

Ingredients:

- 1 oz. butter or olive oil for greasing the baking dish
- 1 ½ lbs. salmon or white fish
- Salt and pepper
- 4 tbsps. butter or ghee
- 2 tbsps. red curry paste or green curry paste
- 14 oz. coconut cream
- 8 tbsps. fresh cilantro, chopped
- 1 lb. cauliflower or broccoli

Directions:

1. Set the oven's temperature to 400°F (200°C). Butter a baking pan.
2. Put the pieces in a medium-sized baking dish; the wall of the dish should not be too far away from the fish.
3. To taste, add salt and pepper. Each piece of fish should have a tablespoon of butter on top.
4. In a small dish, combine the coconut cream, curry paste, and cilantro, then spoon the mixture over the fish.
5. Fish should be cooked after 20 minutes in the oven.
6. Serve the fish with the cauliflower or broccoli that has been briefly blanched in gently salted water.

Nutritional Information:

Calories: 355

Fat: 21 g

Carbohydrates: 3 g

Protein: 37 g

78. Blue Cheese Casserole

Preparation Time: 20 minutes

Cooking Time: 40 minutes

Servings: 4

Ingredients:

- 2 oz. butter
- 1 lb. ground beef
- 1 yellow onion, finely chopped
- 7 oz. fresh green beans
- 5 oz. blue cheese
- 1 c. heavy whipping cream
- 4 oz. shredded cheddar cheese
- Salt and pepper
- 5 oz. leafy greens
- 4 tbsps. olive oil

Directions:

1. Set the oven's temperature to 400°F (200°C).
2. The beans should be trimmed and divided into bite-sized pieces. Over medium-high heat, brown the beef, onion, and butter until the meat is thoroughly cooked.
3. Beans should be added at the end. Stir in the blue cheese crumbs.
4. Bring to a simmer after adding the heavy cream. To taste, add salt and pepper to the food.
5. Add to a baking dish that has been buttered. Add some cheese shavings on top. Bake in the oven for 15 to 20 minutes or until golden brown.
6. Olive oil and leafy greens should be served.

Nutritional Information:

Calories: 355

Fat: 21 g

Carbohydrates: 3 g

Protein: 37 g

79. Barbeque Bacon Chicken Casserole

Preparation Time: 20 minutes

Cooking Time: 40 minutes

Servings: 4

Ingredients:

- 2 lb. cooked chicken breasts diced
- 20 oz. bag of frozen cauliflower thawed and drained well
- 6 oz. cream cheese softened
- ½ c. mayo
- ½ c. sour cream
- 8 oz. cheddar cheese shredded or cubed, divided
- 2 tsps. garlic powder
- 2 tsps. onion powder
- 2 tsps. smoked paprika
- 1 tsp. Salt
- ½ tsp. Pepper
- ⅛ tsp. Chipotle powder
- ⅛ tsp. Dried rosemary
- ⅛ tsp. Dried thyme
- ½ c. + 2 tbsps. Bacon crumbles divided

Directions:

1. Combine the seasonings, mayonnaise, cream cheese, and sour cream. Be sure to combine thoroughly.
2. Half the bacon, the chicken, the cauliflower, and ¾ of the cheese should be incorporated.
3. Place inside a casserole dish. The remaining cheese and bacon are sprinkled on top.
4. After 35 to 40 minutes of bubbling, hot baking at 350°F.

Nutritional Information:

Calories: 355

Fat: 21 g

Carbohydrates: 3 g

Protein: 37 g

Chapter 4:
Vegetable Recipes

80. Spinach and Artichoke Dip Casserole

Preparation Time: 20 minutes

Cooking Time: 40 minutes

Servings: 4

Ingredients:

- 4 c. raw cauliflower florets, roughly chopped
- ¼ c. butter
- ½ c. Silk Cashew Milk, Unsweetened Original
- 8 oz. full-fat cream cheese
- ½ tsp. kosher salt
- ⅛ tsp. ground black pepper
- ¼ tsp. ground nutmeg
- ¼ tsp. garlic powder
- ¼ tsp. smoked paprika (use regular if you can't find smoked)
- 1 c. frozen, chopped spinach
- ¾ c. canned or frozen artichoke hearts, drained and chopped
- 1 ½ c. shredded whole milk mozzarella cheese
- ¼ c. grated parmesan cheese

Directions:

1. Simmer the cauliflower in a saucepan on the stove until the cauliflower is just fork-tender.
2. Add the spinach, artichoke hearts, 1 cup of shredded mozzarella, and parmesan cheese to the cauliflower mixture and stir gently to combine thoroughly.
3. Spoon the mixture into an ovenproof casserole dish and sprinkle the remaining ½ cup of mozzarella over the top.
4. Bake for 20 minutes at 400°F or until golden and bubbling.
5. Serve hot.

Nutritional Information:

Calories: 355

Fat: 21 g

Carbohydrates: 3 g

Protein: 37 g

81. Italian Zucchini Bake Casserole

Preparation Time: 20 minutes

Cooking Time: 40 minutes

Servings: 4

Ingredients:

- 2 tsps. canola oil
- 2 lb. zucchini, cut into ¼-inch half-moon slices
- ¼ c. chopped onion
- 3 plum tomatoes, cut into ½-inch chunks
- 1 tbsp. Parmesan cheese
- ½ c. shredded Italian blend cheese
- 1 tsp. garlic powder
- 1 tsp. Italian seasoning
- ¼ tsp. black pepper
- 1 tbsp. Italian bread crumbs

Directions:

1. Bake at 375°F. Apply cooking spray to a 2-quart baking dish.
2. Zucchini and onion should be sauteed for 5 minutes in a skillet with oil heated to medium-high heat. The blend of black pepper, Italian seasoning, garlic powder, Parmesan cheese, and Italian cheese should all be mixed.
3. Cook for 3 minutes. Add bread crumbs after spooning them into the baking dish that has been prepared.
4. Until brown and thoroughly cooked, bake for 25 to 30 minutes.

Nutritional Information:

Calories: 165

Carbohydrate: 3.8 g

Protein: 9.2 g

Sodium: 797 mg

Potassium: 193 mg

Phosphorus: 202.5 mg

Dietary Fiber: 0.7 g

Fat: 15.22 g

82. Egg White Casserole

Preparation Time: 20 minutes

Cooking Time: 40 minutes

Servings: 4

Ingredients:

- ½ lb. lean ground turkey breast
- ½ red bell pepper, diced
- ½ c. diced onion
- ⅛ tsp. Salt
- ⅛ tsp. black pepper
- 4 egg whites
- 3 eggs
- ¼ c. skim milk
- 1 tsp. Dry mustard
- ½ tsp. garlic powder
- 2 c. spinach

Directions:

1. Set oven to 375°F. Spray cooking oil in an 8 × 8-inch baking dish.
2. Cook the turkey, bell peppers, onions, salt, and black pepper in a skillet coated with cooking spray for 4-5 minutes or until the turkey is no longer pink. Place aside.
3. Egg whites, eggs, milk, dry mustard, and garlic powder should all be whisked together in a big basin. Add spinach and meat mixture after mixing. Put into the baking pan.
4. The egg should be set after 30-35 minutes of baking. Serve squares right away after cutting.

Nutritional Information:

Calories: 183

Carbohydrate: 17.9 g

Protein: 0.3 g

Sodium: 2 g

Potassium: 100 mg

Phosphorus: 12.5 mg

Dietary Fiber: 1.4 g

Fat: 14.17 g

83. Italian Eggplant Casserole

Preparation Time: 20 minutes

Cooking Time: 40 minutes

Servings: 4

Ingredients:

- 1 (1 lb.) eggplant, peeled, cubed
- ½ c. seasoned bread crumbs, divided
- ½ c. liquid egg substitute
- ½ tsp. Garlic powder
- ¼ tsp. Italian seasoning
- ⅛tsp. Black pepper
- ⅛ tsp. salt
- 2 tomatoes, sliced

Directions:

1. Bring 2 inches of water to a boil in a soup pot. Add the eggplant, cover, and simmer for 20 to 30 minutes until tender. Drain.
2. Set oven to 350°F. Spray cooking spray in a 9-inch square baking dish.
3. With a fork, mash the eggplant in a medium basin. Add the egg substitute, Italian seasoning, garlic, salt, pepper, and ¼ cup of bread crumbs.
4. Slices of tomato should be placed on the spread eggplant mixture in the baking dish. Cooking spray is applied to the tomatoes before the remaining bread crumbs are added.
5. Bake for 25 to 30 minutes or until the tomatoes are soft and the edges are browned.

Nutritional Information:

Calories: 220

Carbohydrate: 2.59 g

Protein: 3.2 g

Sodium: 288 mg

Potassium: 133.5 mg

Phosphorus: 68.5 mg

Dietary Fiber: 1.7 g

Fat: 23.7 g

84. Sweet Potato Casserole

Preparation Time: 10 minutes

Cooking Time: 40 minutes

Servings: 4

Ingredients:

- 3 c. baked sweet potatoes, mashed
- ½ c. Splenda
- 3 egg whites
- 2 tbsps. of 'Light I Can't Believe It's Not Butter'
- ¼ c. unsweetened Almond milk
- 1 tsp. vanilla extract

For the Topping:

- ¼ c. packed Splenda brown sugar
- ⅔ c. chopped pecans
- 1 tbsp. all-purpose flour
- 3 tbsps. 'Light I Can't Believe It's Not Butter, softened.'

Directions:

1. Set oven to 350°F (175°C). Cooking spray should be used to coat a 2-quart baking pan.
2. The mashed sweet potatoes, Splenda, egg whites, Light 'I Can't Believe It's Not Butter', almond milk, and vanilla extract should all be combined in a medium bowl. Spread evenly into the baking dish that has been prepared.
3. Combine the brown sugar, finely chopped pecans, flour, and ¼ cup of softened butter in a separate basin. Over the sweet potato mixture, spread evenly.
4. Bake for 35 minutes, or until a knife inserted close to the center comes out clean, in a preheated oven.

Nutritional Information: Calories: 220, Carbohydrate: 2.59 g, Protein: 3.2 g , Sodium: 288 mg , Potassium: 133.5 mg , Phosphorus: 68.5 mg , Dietary Fiber: 1.7 g , Fat: 23.7 g

85. Cabbage Casserole

Preparation Time: 20 minutes

Cooking Time: 40 minutes

Servings: 4

Ingredients:

- 14 oz. Classic Cole Slaw Mix (Dole works well)
- 22 oz. Beef, ground, 80% lean meat / 20% fat, patty, cooked, broiled [hamburger, ground round]
- 1 ½ c. Tomato Sauce
- 2 servings of 'Hunts' Diced Tomatoes w/ Basil, Garlic, and Oregano
- ¼ c., chopped Onions, raw
- 2 c. Part Skim Mozzarella Shredded Cheese
- 1 c. Green Giant Riced Cauliflower
- 2 tbsps. Paprika

Directions:

1. 1 to 1.5 lb. of ground beef and ¼ cup of onion are browned and drained. Add 1 to 2 cups of riced cauliflower, a can of tomato sauce, diced tomato, salt, pepper, and paprika.
2. Cook the cole slaw mixture until tender in a different pan.
3. Spray Pam in a casserole dish, layer meat mixture over sauteed cole slaw mixture, top with mozzarella, and bake at 385 °F for 10 to 15 minutes, or until cheese has melted and the dish is beginning to bubble. Before serving, give it a few minutes to sit.

Nutritional Information:

Calories: 220

Carbohydrate: 2.59 g

Protein: 3.2 g

Sodium: 288 mg

Potassium: 133.5 mg

Phosphorus: 68.5 mg

Dietary Fiber: 1.7 g

Fat: 23.7 g

86. Artichoke Rice Salad

Preparation Time: 10 minutes

Cooking Time: 10 minutes

Servings: 4

Ingredients:

- 2 c. chicken broth
- 1 c. uncooked regular rice
- ¼ c. chopped green onion
- ¼ c. chopped green bell pepper
- ¼ c. pimento-stuffed green olives
- 6 oz. Jar marinated artichoke hearts drained
- ½ c. mayonnaise
- ¼ tsp. Dried dill
- ½ tsp. Salt
- ¼ tsp. black pepper

Directions:

1. Artichoke hearts should be chopped into bite-sized pieces. Add the chicken broth to a saucepan set over medium heat. Rice is added after bringing the soup to a boil.
2. Turn the heat down to low and cover the pan. Rice should be simmered for 15 to 20 minutes or until it is soft.
3. When ready, the majority of the liquid ought to be absorbed. Before using, let the rice cool and remove the pan from the heat.
4. In a serving bowl, combine the cooled rice, green onion, green bell pepper, green olives, artichoke hearts, mayonnaise, dill, salt, and black pepper. Stir thoroughly to mix. Cover the bowl and chill the salad when you're ready to serve.
5. Serve the salad in lettuce leaves if desired.

Nutritional Information: Calories: 232 , Total Fat: 7.8 g , Saturated Fat: 1 g , Cholesterol: 0 mg , Total Carbs: 32.7 g , Sugar: 6.4 g , Fiber: 9.3 g , Sodium: 132 mg , Potassium: 566 mg , Protein: 10 g

87. Brussels Sprouts and Rice

Preparation Time: 20 minutes

Cooking Time: 30 minutes

Servings: 4

Ingredients:

- 10.75 oz. can cream of celery soup
- 1 c. whole milk
- 1 c. water
- 1 tbsp. unsalted butter
- 1 tsp. salt
- ⅔ c. uncooked rice
- 2 packages (10 oz.) of frozen brussels sprouts

Directions:

1. Add the cream of celery soup, milk, water, unsalted butter, and salt to a big saucepan. Up until the mixture starts to boil, stir continuously. After adding the rice, cover the pan with a lid. For 15 minutes, simmer over low heat.
2. Add the Brussels sprouts and stir. Recover the lid, then let the food simmer for 15 minutes. Both the rice and the brussels sprouts should be soft.

Nutritional Information:

Calories: 204

Total fat: 6 g

Saturated fat: 1 g

Cholesterol: 141 mg

Sodium: 223 mg

Carbohydrates: 29 g

Fiber: 1 g

Phosphorus: 120 mg

Potassium: 147 mg

Protein: 8 g

88. Chantilly Rice

Preparation Time: 20 minutes

Cooking Time: 40 minutes

Servings: 4

Ingredients:

- 3 c. cooked rice
- ¾ c. shredded cheddar cheese
- ½ c. sour cream
- 3 dashes of Tabasco sauce

Directions:

1. Preheat the oven to 350°. Spray a 1 ½ quart casserole dish with nonstick cooking spray. Add the rice, ½ cup of cheddar cheese, sour cream, and Tabasco sauce to the casserole dish. Stir until combined.
2. Place a lid on the casserole dish or cover the dish with aluminum foil. Bake for 20 minutes. Remove the lid and sprinkle ¼ cup of cheddar cheese over the top of the rice. Bake for 5 minutes. Remove the dish from the oven and serve.

Nutritional Information:

Calories: 127

Fat: 10 g

Carbohydrates: 8 g

Protein: 4 g

89. Chick Pea Curry Rice Salad

Preparation Time: 20 minutes

Cooking Time: 1 hour

Servings: 6

Ingredients:

For the Salad:

- 2 c. cooked brown rice
- 1 tsp. ground cumin
- ½ cup raisins
- 1 can chickpeas rinsed and drained
- ⅔ c. red onion finely chopped
- 1 red bell pepper cored, seeded, and chopped
- 1 c. cilantro or parsley chopped

For the Baked Tofu:

- 1 container firm organic tofu, drained and pressed for 30 minutes
- ¼ c. soy sauce or Tamari
- 2 tbsps. maple syrup
- ¼ tsp garlic powder
- 2 tbsps. ketchup
- Ground black pepper to taste
- 1 tbsp. rice vinegar
- A dash of hot sauce

For the Dressing:

- 4 tsps. Apple cider vinegar
- ½ tsp. sea salt
- 4 tsps. curry powder
- 4 tsps. lime juice
- 4 tsps. maple syrup

Directions:

For the Baked Tofu:

1. Set the oven to 375F. A baking sheet can be lightly sprayed with oil or lined with parchment paper.
2. With a tofu press or something similar (like a heavy object), press the tofu for 15 minutes.
3. Make 1" cubes of tofu.
4. Mix the soy sauce, maple syrup, ketchup, vinegar, spicy sauce, garlic powder, and black pepper in a small bowl.

5. Stir the tofu cubes gently into the marinade, cover, and let it sit for at least 10 minutes.
6. On the baking sheet, place the tofu in a single layer, bake for 15 minutes, then turn it over and bake for another 15 minutes or until golden brown.

For the Rice Salad:

1. The dressing's components—vinegar, lime juice, curry powder, maple syrup, and salt—must be combined in a small basin.
2. Cooked rice, raisins, cumin, chickpeas, bell pepper, onion, and cilantro should all be added to a big bowl and mixed together.
3. Add the dressing and stir thoroughly.

Nutritional Information:

Calories: 264

Fat: 4.6 g

Total Carbs: 46.9 g

Sugar: 14.2 g

Fiber: 7.7 g

Sodium: 334.4 mg

Protein: 11.7 g

90. Confetti Rice Salad

Preparation Time: 10 minutes

Cooking Time: 40 minutes

Servings: 4

Ingredients:

- 10 oz. package of frozen green peas
- 2 c. cooked rice
- 1 zucchini, shredded
- 2 tbsps. chopped red pimento
- ⅔ c. vegetable oil
- 3 tbsps. Vinegar
- ½ tsp. Salt
- ¼ tsp. Granulated sugar
- ¼ tsp. dried basil

Directions:

1. In a saucepan over medium heat, add the green peas. Cover the peas with water and cook for about 10 minutes. The peas should be done but tender. Remove the pan from the heat and drain all the water from the peas. Rinse the peas with cold water and drain again.
2. Add the green peas, rice, zucchini, red pimento, vegetable oil, vinegar, salt, granulated sugar, and basil to a mixing bowl. Toss until well combined. Let the rice and vegetables sit for 5 minutes at room temperature. Drain the liquid from the salad before serving.
3. You can refrigerate the salad until the serving time is desired. The salad is best served at room temperature. Serve the rice on lettuce leaves if desired.

Nutritional Information: Calories: 228, Total Fat: 13.2 g, Saturated Fat: 3 g , Cholesterol: 248 mg, Total Carbs: 21.3 g , Sugar: 16.1 g , Fiber: 3.8 g, Sodium: 145 mg, Potassium: 251 mg, Protein: 8.8 g

91. Crab Wild Rice Salad

Preparation Time: 20 minutes

Cooking Time: 40 minutes

Servings: 4

Ingredients:

- ½ c. uncooked wild rice
- 1 ½ c. water
- 12 oz. fresh cooked crab meat, flaked
- 2 hard-boiled eggs, chopped
- 1 c. chopped celery
- ¼ c. + 2 tbsps. Chopped onion
- ¼ c. + 2 tbsps. chopped red bell pepper
- ¼ c. sweet pickle relish
- ½ c. plain yogurt
- ¼ c. mayonnaise
- 1 tsp. lemon juice
- 8 oz. fresh snow peas

Directions:

1. In hot water, wash the wild rice three times. Ensure the wild rice is well rinsed because the grains will contain dirt particles. Wild rice and water should be placed in a saucepan over medium heat. The rice should boil.
2. Turn the heat down to low and cover the pan. Rice should be cooked for around 45 minutes or until it is soft. With a fork, fluff the rice after taking the pan from the heat.
3. Rice, crab meat, eggs, celery, onion, red bell pepper, sweet pickle relish, yogurt, mayonnaise, and lemon juice should all be combined in a mixing dish.
4. Gently blend by gently tossing. For 3 hours, refrigerate the bowl with its cover on. The salad needs to be well-cooled.
5. Cook the snow peas just before the rice is almost cold. Add the snow peas to a saucepan over medium heat.
6. Boil the peas for about 2 minutes with a lid on. Drain all the water from the pan and turn off the heat. Drain the water again after giving the snow peas a cold water rinse.
7. The snow peas should be put on a serving plate. To serve, spoon the rice salad over the snow peas.

Nutritional Information: Calories: 184, Fat: 15 g, Carbohydrates: 1 g, Protein: 12 g

92. Creole Boiled Rice

Preparation Time: 10 minutes

Cooking Time: 30 minutes

Servings: 4

Ingredients:

- 3 qt. water
- 3 tbsps. unsalted butter
- 1 tbsp. salt
- 2 c. long grain rice, uncooked
- Cayenne pepper and Tabasco sauce to taste

Directions:

1. Add the water, 3 tablespoons of butter, and salt to a sizable saucepan set over medium heat. Water is brought to a boil. Add the rice when the water is boiling.
2. Cook the rice for about 15-20 minutes, or until it is cooked, on medium-low heat. After taking the rice off the heat, drain any water that may have remained.
3. Cayenne and Tabasco sauce can be used to season food to taste. Before serving, fluff the rice with a fork.

Nutritional Information:

Calories: 394

Carbs: 11 g

Protein: 29 g

Fat: 28 g

Phosphorus: 316 mg

Potassium: 745 mg

Sodium: 252 mg

93. Curried Rice Salad

Preparation Time: 20 minutes

Cooking Time: 50 minutes

Servings: 4

Ingredients:

- 2 c. cooked brown rice, chilled
- ½ c. finely chopped celery
- ¼ c. grated carrot
- ¼ c. cooked green peas
- ½ c. mayonnaise
- ¼ c. plain yogurt
- 1 tsp. lemon juice
- ½ tsp. curry powder
- 4 large lettuce leaves

Directions:

1. In a mixing bowl, add the brown rice, celery, carrot, green peas, mayonnaise, yogurt, lemon juice, and curry powder. Stir until well combined.
2. When ready to serve, place the lettuce leaves on a serving platter. Spoon the rice salad in equal portions onto the center of the lettuce leaves.

Nutritional Information:

Calories: 605

Fat: 46 g

Carbohydrates: 6 g

Protein: 39 g

94. Madras Rice Salad

Preparation Time: 10 minutes

Cooking Time: 30 minutes

Servings: 4

Ingredients:

- 2 c. cooked rice
- 10 oz. package of frozen green peas, thawed
- 2 tomatoes, peeled, seeded, and chopped
- ⅓ c. olive oil
- ¼ c. minced onion
- ¼ c. minced fresh parsley
- 3 tbsps. white wine vinegar
- 1 tbsp. Minced fresh basil
- ¼ tsp. Salt
- ¼ tsp. black pepper

Directions:

1. In a serving bowl, add all the ingredients. Toss until well combined. Cover the bowl and refrigerate for 3 hours before serving. The salad needs to be well chilled before serving.
2. Toss the salad again before serving.

Nutritional Information:

Calories: 228

Total Fat: 13.2 g

Saturated Fat: 3 g

Cholesterol: 248 mg

Total Carbs: 21.3 g

Sugar: 16.1 g

Fiber: 3.8 g

Sodium: 145 mg

Potassium: 251 mg

Protein: 8.8 g

95. Pine Nut Rice and Feta Salad

Preparation Time: 10 minutes

Cooking Time: 10 minutes

Servings: 4

Ingredients:

- 6 oz. package of long grain and wild rice mix prepared
- 4 oz. crumbled Feta cheese
- ½ c. chopped green bell pepper
- ½ c. chopped yellow bell pepper
- ½ c. chopped onion
- 2 oz. jar of diced red pimentos, drained
- ⅓ c. olive oil
- 2 tbsps. tarragon wine vinegar
- ⅛ tsp. black pepper

Directions:

1. The wild rice mix should be prepared and cooled before making this salad.
2. In a mixing bowl, add the Feta cheese, green bell pepper, yellow bell pepper, onion, red pimentos, and rice. Gently toss until combined.
3. Whisk together the olive oil, tarragon, wine vinegar, and black pepper in a small bowl. Pour the dressing over the rice.
4. Gently toss until well combined. Cover the bowl and chill the salad no longer than 24 hours before serving.

Nutritional Information:

Calories: 212

Fat: 15.8 g

Carbohydrates: 12.1 g

Protein: 8.6 g

96. Vegetable Rice Salad

Preparation Time: 20 minutes

Cooking Time: 40 minutes

Servings: 4

Ingredients:

- 3 c. cold cooked rice
- 1 cucumber, peeled and chopped
- 1 large carrot, peeled and diced
- 1 c. fresh green beans, cut into 1" pieces
- 1 c. frozen green peas
- 1 red bell pepper, chopped
- 2 tomatoes, peeled, seeded, and cut into strips
- 2 tbsps. tarragon vinegar
- 1 tsp. salt
- ½ tsp. black pepper
- ¼ c. + 2 tbsps. olive oil
- 6 lettuce leaves
- Additional salt and black pepper to taste

Directions:

1. In a mixing bowl, add the cucumber. Sprinkle the cucumber with ½ teaspoon of salt. Cover the bowl and let the cucumber sit for 30 minutes at room temperature.
2. Rinse the cucumber and drain well. Do not skip this step. The flavor of the cucumber adds an element to the rice that is not available unless the cucumber sits in salt.
3. In a saucepan over medium heat, add the carrot, green beans, and green peas. Cover the vegetables with water. Cook for about 8-10 minutes or until the vegetables are crisp-tender.
4. Remove the pan from the heat and drain all the water from the vegetables. Rinse the vegetables with cold water to cool them.
5. Add the vegetables to the cucumber in the bowl. Stir in the red bell pepper, rice, and tomatoes in the bowl. Whisk together the tarragon vinegar, ½ teaspoon salt, black pepper, and olive oil in a small bowl. Whisk until well combined.
6. Pour the dressing over the vegetables and rice. Toss until all the ingredients are coated with the dressing. Spoon the salad over lettuce leaves to serve.
7. Season to taste with salt and black pepper if desired.

Nutritional Information: Calories: 232, Total Fat: 7.8 g, Saturated Fat: 1 g, Cholesterol: 0 mg, Total Carbs: 32.7 g, Sugar: 6.4 g , Fiber: 9.3 g, Sodium: 132 mg, Potassium: 566 mg, Protein: 10 g

97. Waldorf Rice

Preparation Time: 10 minutes

Cooking Time: 34 minutes

Servings: 4

Ingredients:

- ½ c. chopped onion
- 2 tbsps. unsalted butter
- 2 c. apple juice
- ⅓ c. water
- ½ tsp. salt
- 1 c. uncooked regular rice
- 2 apples, chopped
- 1 c. sliced celery
- ½ c. chopped walnuts
- ½ tsp. rum extract

Directions:

1. Place the onion and butter in a large saucepan set over medium heat for 4 minutes in hot oil. Add salt, water, and apple juice after stirring.
2. Rice is added after bringing the juice to a boil. Turn the heat down to low and cover the pan. The rice should simmer for 20 minutes.
3. Add the apples, celery, walnuts, and rum essence after stirring. After serving, turn off the heat in the pan.

Nutritional Information:

Calories: 127

Fat: 10 g

Carbohydrates: 8 g

Protein: 4 g

98. Wild Rice and Beef Loaf

Preparation Time: 10 minutes

Cooking Time: 45 minutes

Servings: 4

Ingredients:

- ⅓ c. long grain and wild rice mixed with 2 tsps. seasoning mix prepared
- ¼ c. chopped onion
- 1 tbsp. unsalted butter
- 3 oz. can chopped mushrooms, drained
- 3 eggs, beaten
- 1 tsp. Worcestershire sauce
- 2 tbsps. seasoned bread crumbs
- 2 lbs. ground beef
- 1 ½ tsps. salt

Directions:

1. In a skillet over medium-low heat, add the onion and butter. Saute the onion for 3 minutes. Add the mushrooms and stir until well combined. Remove the skillet from the heat.
2. Add 1 egg, Worcestershire sauce, rice, and onion in a small bowl. Stir until well combined. Set the bowl aside for the moment.
3. Add the ground beef, 2 eggs, bread crumbs, and salt in a large mixing bowl. Using your hands, mix until well combined. Preheat the oven to 350°. Place ⅓ of the meat mixture in the bottom of a loaf pan.
4. Spoon half of the rice mixture over the meat. Repeat with ⅓ meat mixture and the remaining rice mixture. Press the remaining meat mixture over the top layer of rice. Press the mixture well into the loaf pan so the flavors will blend.
5. Bake for 1 to 1 ½ hours or until the beef is done and no longer pink. Drain off the excess grease. Let the meatloaf sit for 10 minutes before serving.

Nutritional Information: Calories: 394, Carbs: 11 g, Protein: 29 g, Fat: 28 g, Phosphorus: 316 mg, Potassium: 745 mg, Sodium: 252 mg

99. Pebble Salad

Preparation Time: 10 minutes

Cooking Time: 10 minutes

Servings: 4

Ingredients:

- 6 oz. package of long grain and wild rice mix prepared
- 12 oz. can white corn, drained
- 1 c. cucumber, chopped
- 2 carrots, chopped
- ¼ c. sliced green onions
- ⅓ c. chopped fresh parsley
- ¼ c. olive oil
- ¼ c. lemon juice
- 1 garlic clove, minced
- ½ tsp. dried dill
- ¼ tsp. dry mustard
- ⅛ tsp. black pepper
- ½ c. roasted sunflower kernels
- 8 large lettuce leaves

Directions:

1. The cooked rice, corn, cucumber, carrots, green onions, and parsley should all be combined in a sizable bowl. Toss to blend.
2. Olive oil, lemon juice, garlic, dill, dry mustard, and black pepper should all be combined in a small bowl. Blend thoroughly by whisking.
3. Over the items in the bowl, drizzle the dressing. Mix gently until well-combined. For 3 hours, refrigerate the bowl with its cover on.
4. One lettuce leaf should be placed on each serving plate when ready to serve. Each lettuce leaf should have an equal amount of rice salad on top of it. Over the top, scatter the sunflower seeds.

Nutritional Information:

Calories: 212

Fat: 15.8 g

Carbohydrates: 12.1 g

Protein: 8.6 g

100. Brown Rice and Vegetable Salad

Preparation Time: 10 minutes

Cooking Time: 10 minutes

Servings: 4

Ingredients:

- 1 c. uncooked brown rice
- Water
- ½ c. chopped carrot
- 1 c. fresh green beans, cut into 1" pieces
- 1 c. frozen green peas
- 1 cucumber, peeled and chopped
- 1 red bell pepper, chopped
- 1 large tomato, peeled and chopped
- ⅓ c. toasted sunflower seeds
- 1 c. shredded Monterey Jack cheese
- ¼ c. Italian salad dressing
- 3 tbsps. tarragon vinegar
- 2 tbsps. olive oil
- ½ tsp. Coarse ground black pepper

Directions:

1. Rinse the brown rice in cold water until the water runs clear. I always rinse brown rice before cooking it in cold water.
2. Pour 4 cups of water into a sizable saucepan set over medium heat. Rice is added after bringing the water to a boil. For around 30 minutes, cook the rice uncovered.
3. After turning off the heat, cover the rice in the pan with a tight-fitting lid. Give the rice 15 minutes to steam. With a fork, fluff the rice after removing the lid. Rice should be chilled before use.
4. Add the carrot, green beans, and peas to a saucepan over medium heat. When the vegetables are at a boil, cover them with cold water. Turn the heat down to low and cover the pan. The vegetables should be simmered for about 10 minutes or until they are crisp and tender.
5. After turning off the heat, drain the vegetables' water completely. Give the vegetables 10 minutes to cool.
6. Rice, carrots, green beans, green peas, cucumber, red bell pepper, tomato, sunflower seeds, and Monterey Jack cheese should all be combined in a serving bowl. Italian dressing, tarragon vinegar, olive oil, and black pepper should all be combined in a small bowl. Blend thoroughly by whisking.
7. Over the rice and vegetables, drizzle the dressing. When all the ingredients are thoroughly incorporated, toss. Before serving, cover and chill the bowl.

Nutritional Information:

Calories: 219

Total Fat: 4.5 g

Saturated Fat: 0.6 g

Cholesterol: 0 mg

Total Carbs: 38.2 g

Sugar 0.6: g

Fiber: 5 g

Sodium: 92 mg

Potassium: 1721 mg

Protein: 6.4 g

101. Chutney Rice Salad

Preparation Time: 10 minutes

Cooking Time: 10 minutes

Servings: 4

Ingredients:

- 1 c. uncooked long-grain rice
- 3 c. water
- 1 apple, chopped
- ½ c. chopped celery
- ¼ c. raisins
- 2 tbsps. chopped green onions
- 2 tbsps. chopped toasted pecans
- ¼ c. vegetable oil
- 1 tbsp. Lemon juice
- ¼ c. + 2 tbsps. chutney (use your fruit flavor)
- ¼ tsp. Ground ginger
- ⅛ tsp. black pepper

Directions:

1. Add the water to a saucepan set over medium heat. Stir in the rice as soon as the water begins to boil. Then, turn down the heat to medium-low and cover the pan. Rice should simmer for 15 minutes.
2. Once most of the liquid has been absorbed, the rice ought to be soft. Take the pan off the stove. Give the rice 5 minutes to sit. Drain off any remaining water from the rice, if there is any. With a fork, fluff the rice. Rice should be left to cool.
3. Rice, apple, celery, raisins, green onions, and nuts should all be combined in a sizable bowl. Toss to blend.
4. Mix the vegetable oil, lemon juice, chutney, ginger, and black pepper in another bowl. Ensure that the dressing is thoroughly blended. Over the rice mixture, drizzle the dressing.
5. Gently toss the rice until it is evenly covered in the dressing. Place a cover on the bowl and chill in the refrigerator.

Nutritional Information: Calories: 219, Total Fat: 4.5 g, Saturated Fat: 0.6 g, Cholesterol: 0 mg, Total Carbs: 38.2 g, Sugar: 0.6 g, Fiber: 5 g, Sodium: 92 mg, Potassium: 1721 mg, Protein: 6 g

102. Mandarin Orange Rice Salad

Preparation Time: 10 minutes

Cooking Time: 10 minutes

Servings: 4

Ingredients:

- 2 c. water
- ½ tsp. salt
- 1 c. uncooked long-grain rice
- 11 oz. can mandarin oranges, drained
- ½ c. thinly sliced celery
- ½ c. diced green bell pepper
- 3 tbsps. chopped green onion
- 3 tbsps. lemon juice
- 3 tbsps. Olive oil
- ¼ tsp. black pepper
- 6 lettuce leaves

Directions:

1. In a large saucepan over medium heat, add the water and salt. When the water begins to boil, stir in the rice. Reduce the heat to medium-low and place a lid on the pan.
2. Simmer the rice for 15 minutes or until the rice is tender. Remove the pan from the heat. Let the rice sit for 5 minutes. Remove the lid from the pan and spoon the rice into a serving bowl.
3. Refrigerate the rice until well chilled. Remove 6 mandarin orange slices and set aside. Add the remaining mandarin oranges, celery, green bell pepper, onion, lemon juice, olive oil, and black pepper. Stir until well combined.
4. Place the lettuce leaves on a platter. Spoon the rice salad onto the lettuce leaves. Arrange the reserved 6 mandarin orange slices over the top of the salad.

Nutritional Information: Calories: 186, Total Fat: 3.3 g, Saturated Fat: 0.4 g, Cholesterol: 0 mg, Total Carbs: 32.3 g, Sugar: 2.7 g, Fiber: 4.6 g, Sodium: 25 mg, Potassium: 312 mg, Protein: 6.4 g

103. Rice Salad with Fresh Mushrooms

Preparation Time: 10 minutes

Cooking Time: 10 minutes

Servings: 4

Ingredients:

- 7 oz. package of instant rice
- 5 chicken bouillon cubes
- 1 c. chopped onion
- 1 c. chopped green bell pepper
- 1 c. chopped celery
- 8 oz. fresh mushrooms, sliced
- 4 oz. jar of diced red pimento
- 8 oz. bottle of creamy Italian dressing

Directions:

1. Cook the rice according to package directions, except omit the salt in the package directions. When the rice boils, add the chicken bouillon cubes to the rice. When the rice is tender, drain any remaining liquid from the rice if needed. When the rice is cooked, place the rice in a mixing bowl.
2. Add the onion, green bell pepper, celery, mushrooms, red pimento, and Italian dressing to the rice. Toss until well combined.
3. Cover the bowl and chill thoroughly before serving.

Nutritional Information:

Calories: 137

Total Fat: 6.5 g

Saturated Fat: 0.9 g

Cholesterol: 0 mg

Total Carbs: 16.9 g

Sugar: 0 g

Fiber: 2.6 g

Sodium: 203 mg

Potassium: 158 mg

Protein: 4 g

104. Wild Rice and Kale Bake

Preparation Time: 10 minutes

Cooking Time: 20 minutes

Servings: 4

Ingredients:

- 2 large bunches of kale, torn
- 1 c. water
- 1 lb. mushrooms, sliced
- 3 tbsps. olive oil, divided
- 2 cloves of garlic, minced
- 2 tbsps. Fresh tarragon, chopped
- ¼ tsp. nutmeg
- Salt and pepper to taste
- 4 tbsps. all-purpose flour
- 1 c. milk
- 1 c. vegetable broth
- ¼ c. heavy cream
- 4 c. cooked wild rice
- 1 ½ c. gruyere cheese, shredded

Directions:

1. A 3-quart casserole dish should be greased and left aside. Turn the oven on to 375°F.
2. A fairly large skillet should be heated at medium-high. Water and kale should be added to the skillet. Cook the kale under cover for 10 to 15 minutes, stirring once or twice.
3. The kale should be removed from the skillet, drained of any extra liquid, and kept aside.
4. Add 3 tablespoons of olive oil and bring the skillet back to medium heat. Salt and pepper the mushrooms once they have been browned. Cook for about a minute after adding the garlic, tarragon, and nutmeg. Add the kale and thoroughly combine.
5. After adding the flour, sauté the kale and mushrooms for 1 minute.
6. When the sauce is thick enough, simmer it for 2-3 minutes after adding the milk and stock and bringing it to a boil. Stir in the cream after adding it. Stir in the cooked wild rice after taking the pan off the heat. Fill the casserole dish with the mixture.
7. The casserole should have cheese on it. When the cheese is melted, bake for another 20 to 25 minutes. Serve!

Nutritional Information: Calories: 330, Fat: 16 g, Carbs: 48 g, Protein: 17 g, Sodium: 480 mg

105. Tangy Spinach and Cheese Pasta

Preparation Time: 10 minutes

Cooking Time: 50 minutes

Servings: 4

Ingredients:

- 10 oz. dry rotini pasta
- 1 (5 oz.) package of fresh baby spinach
- 1 tbsp. olive oil
- 2 large onions, diced
- ¼ c. all-purpose flour
- 3 cloves of garlic, minced
- 2 ½ c. milk
- ½ c. dry white wine
- 1 c. Parmesan cheese, grated, divided
- 1 tsp. Salt
- ½ tsp. Black pepper
- ½ tsp. grated lemon rind
- ¾ c. buttery round crackers, crushed

Directions:

1. Preheat the oven to 350°F and coat a 9x13" baking dish with cooking spray.
2. Cook it in boiling water for 8 minutes or until the pasta is almost done. After taking it off the heat, toss in the spinach. Give it a two-minute rest period to allow the spinach to wilt.
3. In the meantime, put the olive oil and onions in a sizable nonstick skillet and heat over medium heat. Stirring constantly; cook for 15 minutes or until golden brown.
4. Add the flour and garlic and cook for 1 minute, stirring with a whisk. Gradually stir in the milk and wine, and cook until the sauce boils and thickens, constantly stirring (about 10 minutes).
5. Stir three-quarters of the cheese, salt, pepper, and lemon rind. Remove the pot from the heat. Add pasta mixture to the onion mixture and toss gently to coat.
6. Spoon the pasta mixture into the baking dish. Sprinkle half the cracker crumbs over the pasta, and top evenly with the remaining quarter cup of cheese. Top with the last of the cracker crumbs.
7. Bake for 50 minutes or until browned and bubbly.

Nutritional Information: Calories: 399, Fat: 10 g, Carbs: 63 g, Protein: 18 g, Sodium: 611 mg

106. Butternut Squash Lasagna

Preparation Time: 10 minutes

Cooking Time: 50 minutes

Servings: 4

Ingredients:

- 1 tbsp. olive oil
- 2 c. chopped onion
- 10 c. baby spinach
- ¾ c. sharp provolone cheese, shredded
- ½ c. chopped fresh flat-leaf parsley
- 1 tsp. salt
- ½ tsp. black pepper
- 1 tsp. oregano
- 2 large eggs
- 2 (15 oz.) containers of 2% cottage cheese
- 3 c. butternut squash, peeled and diced
- 6 c. marinara or pasta sauce
- 12 oven-ready lasagna noodles (no boiling)
- 1 c. fresh Parmesan cheese, grated

Directions:

1. Preheat the oven to 375°F. Coat the bottom and sides of two 8x8" baking dishes with cooking spray.
2. Heat a large Dutch oven over medium-high heat. Add the oil and onion; sauté 4 minutes or until tender.
3. Add the spinach and stir until the spinach wilts. Remove the pot from the heat. In a large bowl, combine the provolone, parsley, salt, pepper, oregano, eggs, and cottage cheese.
4. Put the squash in a microwave-safe basin for 5 minutes, with the lid on, or until tender.
5. In each baking dish, carry out the following actions: Pasta sauce or marinara sauce should cover the bottom of the dish by half a cup. Spread 1 cup of the cheese mixture over the noodles after placing 2 on top of the sauce. Place 1 ½ cups squash cubes and ¾ cup sauce on the cheese mixture.
6. Spread 1 cup of the cheese mixture over the noodles after placing 2 on top of the sauce. Spread ¾ cup of sauce over the cheese mixture after adding 1 ½ cups of the onion mixture.
7. Place 2 noodles over the sauce, then equally distribute 1 cup of marinara over the noodles. Add ½ cup of Parmesan cheese.
8. Wrap foil around each pan. After the first 30 minutes of baking, remove the foil and bake for 30 minutes.

To freeze unbaked lasagna: Prepare through step 8. Cover with plastic wrap, pressing to remove as much air as possible. Wrap with heavy-duty foil. Store in the freezer for up to 2 months.

To prepare frozen unbaked lasagna: Thaw completely in the refrigerator (about 24 hours). Preheat the oven to 375°F. Remove the foil and set it aside. Discard the plastic wrap. Cover the lasagna with the reserved foil; bake at 375° for 1 hour. Uncover and bake for an additional 30 minutes or until bubbly.

Nutritional Information:

Calories: 289

Fat: 13 g

Carbs: 28 g

Protein: 19 g

Sodium: 560 mg

107. Eggplant Parmesan

Preparation Time: 10 minutes

Cooking Time: 60 minutes

Servings: 4

Ingredients:

- 2 large eggs, lightly beaten
- 1 tbsp. water
- 2 c. panko breadcrumbs
- ¼ c. Parmigiano-Reggiano cheese, grated
- 2 (1 lb.) eggplants, peeled and cut crosswise into ½-inch slices

For the Filling:

- ½ c. fresh basil, chopped
- ¼ c. Parmigiano-Reggiano cheese, grated
- ½ tsp. crushed red pepper
- 3 cloves garlic, minced
- 1 tsp. onion powder
- Salt and pepper to taste
- 2 (8 oz.) containers of 2% cottage cheese
- 1 large egg, lightly beaten

For the Topping:

- 4 c. pasta sauce
- 1 ½ c. mozzarella cheese, shredded

Directions:

1. A 9x13" baking dish and two cookie sheets should be prepared with cooking spray and placed in the preheated 375°F oven.
2. Get the eggplant ready. In a small dish, mix the eggs with 1 tablespoon of water. In a second shallow dish, combine the panko and ¼ cup of Parmigiano-Reggiano.
3. Each slice of eggplant is first dipped in the egg mixture, then gently pressed into the panko mixture so the breadcrumbs adhere and any excess is shaken off.
4. On the baking sheets, space the greased eggplant slices 1-inch apart. They should be baked for 30 minutes, turning them once and rotating the oven sheets after 15 minutes or until they are brown.
5. The basil, ¼ cup of Parmigiano-Reggiano cheese, garlic, onion powder, salt, pepper, cottage cheese, and egg go into the filling's preparation.
6. Pour 12 cups of spaghetti sauce into the baking dish to assemble. Over the pasta sauce, arrange half of the eggplant slices.

7. Spread half of the cottage cheese mixture over the sauce, then top with approximately ¾ cup of pasta sauce. Add a third of the mozzarella next. Once more, layer the ingredients, finishing with roughly a cup of pasta sauce.
8. Cooking spray-coated aluminum foil should be used to cover tightly—35 minutes at 375 °F baking. Add the final third of the mozzarella and take off the foil.
9. Bake for 10 minutes or until the cheese has melted and the sauce is bubbling; let cool before serving.

Nutritional Information:

Calories: 318

Fat: 15 g

Carbs: 27 g

Protein: 19 g

Sodium: 655 mg

108. Artichoke and Spinach Casserole

Preparation Time: 15 minutes

Cooking Time: 25 minutes

Servings: 5

Ingredients:

- 2 tbsps. butter
- 1 small onion, diced
- 3 garlic cloves, minced
- 10 oz. frozen spinach, thawed and drained
- 2 c. marinated artichoke hearts, chopped
- Salt and pepper to taste
- 2 eggs
- ¾ c. plain Greek yogurt
- ½ c. mozzarella cheese
- ¼ c. pepper jack cheese
- 3 c. quinoa, cooked (1 c. dry quinoa)
- ¼ c. Parmesan cheese

Directions:

1. Cooking spray should be used to prepare a 2-quart casserole dish, and preheat the oven to 375°F.
2. In a sauté pan with the butter already melted over medium heat, saute the onion and garlic until aromatic, perhaps a few minutes.
3. Add the spinach to the pan after pressing out any extra water. 5 minutes after adding the chopped artichoke hearts, remove them. Add salt and pepper to taste.
4. In the meantime, thoroughly mix the eggs, yogurt, and cheese in a large bowl.
5. The spinach and artichoke mixture should be taken off the stove and given a few minutes to cool before being added to the egg and cheese bowl. Additionally, stir in the cooked quinoa.
6. Put the mixture in the casserole dish and use a spoon to smooth the top. Cook the dish for 30-35 minutes, or until the top is lightly golden brown, after scattering the Parmesan cheese on top. Enjoy warm servings!

Nutritional Information: Calories: 357, Fat: 14 g, Carbs: 34 g, Protein: 27 g, Sodium: 479 mg

109. Green Bean Casserole

Preparation Time: 10 minutes

Cooking Time: 50 minutes

Servings: 4

Ingredients:

For the Fried Onions:

- 3 tbsps. cornstarch
- 3 tbsps. All-purpose flour
- ½ tsp. salt
- 1 medium onion, sliced into thin strips
- Vegetable oil for frying

For the Casserole:

- 2 tbsps. olive oil
- 1 small onion, finely diced
- 2 cloves garlic, minced
- 8 oz. white mushrooms, finely sliced
- 2 c. milk, divided
- 2 tbsps. cornstarch
- 1 lb. fresh green beans, cleaned, trimmed, and steamed
- ½ tsp. Summer
- ½ tsp. celery seed
- Salt and pepper, to taste
- ½ c. Parmesan cheese, grated, divided

Directions:

For the Onions:

1. In a large resealable bag, combine the cornstarch, flour, and salt. Add the onions and shake the bag to combine. Remove the onions from the bag.
2. Fill a large, heavy-bottomed skillet with a quarter inch of vegetable oil. Heat it over medium-high heat until hot and shimmering. When it is hot, shake any excess flour from the onions, and cook them in batches until golden and crispy.
3. Remove them with a slotted spoon and set them aside on a paper towel to drain.

For the Casserole:

1. Preheat the oven to 350°F. In a medium saucepan, heat the olive oil over medium-high heat. Add the diced onion and garlic. Sauté until soft, stirring frequently.
2. Add the mushrooms, and cook until they are soft and tender, stirring for about 2 minutes.

3. Add 1 ¾ cup of milk and the thyme and celery seed. Bring it to a boil.
4. Combine the remaining ¼ cup of milk and 2 tablespoons of cornstarch until smooth.
5. Whisk the slurry into the onion mixture and allow it to come to a boil, and thicken for about 1 minute. Season with salt and pepper to taste.
6. Add the green beans to the sauce and stir to combine. Pour the mixture into a 2-quart casserole dish. Top with half the grated Parmesan cheese, and cover with foil. Bake for 30 minutes.
7. Remove the foil. Sprinkle the fried onions and remaining cheese over the top of the casserole. Return it to the oven until it is bubbling and lightly golden brown, about 7 minutes.

Nutritional Information:

Calories: 143

Fat: 8 g

Carbs: 18 g

Protein: 2 g

Sodium: 1051 mg

110. Mashed Potato Bake

Preparation Time: 15 minutes

Cooking Time: 40 minutes

Servings: 5

Ingredients:

- 3 lb. Yukon gold potatoes, peeled and chopped
- 3 cloves garlic, crushed and chopped
- 2 tsps. Salt, divided
- ½ tsp. black pepper
- 6 oz. cream cheese softened
- ½ c. Parmesan cheese, grated
- ½ c. breadcrumbs
- 2 tbsps. chives, minced

Directions:

1. Spray cooking spray in a 9x9" baking pan and preheat the oven to 350°F.
2. In a large saucepan, combine the potatoes, garlic, and ½ teaspoon salt. Add water to cover. It should boil. Stirring occasionally simmers for 15 minutes or until fork-tender. ½ cup of the cooking liquid should be set aside while you drain in a colander over a bowl.
3. A ricer pushes the potato pieces (and garlic) into a big basin. Add the cream cheese, the remaining 1 ½ teaspoons of salt and pepper, and the leftover boiling liquid.
4. Put the baking dish with the potato mixture inside. Bake for 20 minutes or until heated all the way through.
5. Set the broiler to high. Bread crumbs and Parmesan combined, then distributed evenly over the potatoes. 4 minutes of broiling or until golden brown. Add a few chives.

Nutritional Information:

Calories: 243

Fat: 7 g

Carbs: 38 g

Protein: 8 g

Sodium: 361 mg

111. Savory Mushroom Bread Pudding

Preparation Time: 15 minutes

Cooking Time: 20 minutes

Servings: 5

Ingredients:

- 7 c. cubed sourdough bread (1-inch cubes)
- 1 ½ c. milk
- ½ c. heavy cream
- 1 small celery root (about 12 oz.), peeled and cut into ½-inch pieces (about 2 c.)
- Salt and pepper to taste
- ½ tsp. Paprika
- ½ tsp. onion powder
- 2 tbsps. butter
- 1 lb. mushrooms, such as shiitake, maitake, cremini, and oyster, thinly sliced
- 1 clove of garlic, minced
- ¼ c. white wine
- 2 large eggs, lightly beaten
- 1 tbsp. fresh thyme leaves, plus sprigs for garnish
- ½ c. crumbled Feta

Directions:

1. Preheat the oven to 400°F and coat a 2-quart baking dish and a cookie sheet with cooking spray.
2. Arrange the bread cubes on the tray, and toast them until golden, about 10 minutes. (Be careful they don't burn.)
3. In the meantime, mix the celery root, milk, and cream in a small pot. After boiling everything, turn down the heat, cover, and simmer for 10 minutes or until the celery root is fork-tender. Allow it to cool a little.
4. Blend the contents in a blender until it is smooth. Add paprika, onion powder, salt, and pepper for seasoning.
5. Melt the butter over medium-high heat in a large skillet. Add the mushrooms and simmer, turning periodically, for about 9 minutes, or until they have mainly shed their moisture and turned golden. After adding the garlic, stir for a minute.
6. With a wooden spoon, whisk in the wine while incorporating any browned bits. Toss the mixture in a bowl after adding salt and pepper to taste. Whisk together the celery root mixture, eggs, and thyme leaves in a large bowl.
7. Fold in the toasted bread and mushrooms. Transfer the casserole to the prepared dish, and sprinkle it with cheese. Garnish with thyme sprigs and bake until the custard is set and the top is lightly browned, about 25 minutes. Let it cool slightly before serving.

Nutritional Information:

Calories: 282

Fat: 14 g

Carbs: 23 g

Protein: 18 g

Sodium: 633 mg

112. Spinach Pasta Casserole

Preparation Time: 15 minutes

Cooking Time: 30 minutes

Servings: 5

Ingredients:

- 12 oz. spinach pasta
- 5 oz. fresh baby spinach
- 2 large shallots, peeled and chopped
- 3 cloves garlic, minced
- 2 oz. Feta cheese, crumbled
- ½ c. low-fat Greek yogurt
- ½ sour c. cream
- ½ c. basil pesto
- Black pepper to taste
- 1 large egg

Directions:

1. An 8x8" baking dish should be lightly greased with cooking spray and placed in a 350°F oven. Pasta made from spinach is added to a pot of boiling, salted water.
2. Cook as directed on the packet, drain, and set aside.
3. In the meantime, put the chopped spinach, shallots, and garlic in a big bowl. Add the Feta cheese and toss.
4. Combine the yogurt, sour cream, and pesto in another bowl. To taste, add black pepper. Add the egg and whisk.
5. Spinach and shallots are combined with the cooked pasta in a bowl. Add the sauce and coat with a toss. Spread it in the baking dish you've prepared or cover it and store it in the fridge for the following day.
6. Bake for 30 minutes or until the top is softly bubbling and golden. After cooling for 10 minutes, serve.

Nutritional Information: Calories: 852, Fat: 59 g, Carbs: 27 g, Protein: 26 g, Sodium: 953 mg

113. Traditional Sweet Potato Casserole

Preparation Time: 15 minutes

Cooking Time: 59 minutes

Servings: 5

Ingredients:

- 2 ½ lbs. sweet potatoes, peeled and cut into 1-inch cubes
- ¾ c. packed brown sugar
- ¼ c. butter softened
- 1 ½ tsps. salt
- 1 tsp. vanilla extract
- ½ c. finely chopped pecans, divided
- 2 c. white miniature marshmallows

Directions:

1. Cooking spray should be used to coat a 7x11" casserole dish before preheating the oven to 375°F.
2. Fill a Dutch oven with cool water, then add the sweet potatoes. They should be brought to a boil, then simmered for 15 minutes or until very soft. Drain, then let it cool a bit.
3. The potatoes should be put in a big bowl. Add the vanilla, salt, butter, sugar, and cream.
4. Use a potato masher to mash the sweet potato mixture, then stir in ¼ cup of pecans. Scrape the mixture into the casserole dish in equal layers.
5. Top with marshmallows and the final ¼ cup of pecans.
6. Golden brown after 25 minutes of baking.

Nutritional Information:

Calories: 186

Fat: 6 g

Carbs: 33 g

Protein: 2 g

Sodium: 272 mg

Chapter 5:
Dessert and Sweet Recipes

114. Bakery French Toast

Preparation Time: 15 minutes

Cooking Time: 50 minutes

Servings: 5

Ingredients:

- 1 loaf of day-old bakery cinnamon-raisin bread (14 slices)
- 3 eggs, lightly beaten
- 1 ½ c. half and half
- 1 c. whipping cream
- ½ c. brown sugar
- ½ tsp. vanilla extract
- ½ tsp. ground cinnamon
- Maple syrup for serving

Directions:

1. Turn the oven on to 375°F. Use cooking spray to grease an 8x8" baking pan.
2. 3 bread pieces, trimmed to fit, should be used to line the baking pan's bottom. Add 3 additional slices on top, trimmed to size. 8 slices should be arranged shingle-style across the top in two rows. Apply pressure firmly.
3. Eggs are whisked in a medium bowl. Add the cream, sugar, cinnamon, vanilla, and half-and-half after blending. After uniformly spreading the egg mixture over the bread, securely wrap it in foil.
4. For 40 minutes, bake. Bake for another 10 minutes after removing the foil. 10 minutes should pass before serving. Add maple syrup to the dish.

Nutritional Information:

Calories: 398

Fat: 16 g

Carbs: 54 g

Protein: 10 g

Sodium: 369 mg

115. Apricot Apple Crisp

Preparation Time: 15 minutes

Cooking Time: 20 minutes

Servings: 5

Ingredients:

- 1 tsp. butter for greasing
- 5 Granny Smith apples, sliced
- 1 c. dried apricots, finely chopped
- 1 tbsp. lemon juice
- ⅓ c. brown sugar
- ½ c. all-purpose flour

For the Topping:

- ¾ c. rolled oats
- ¾ c. brown sugar
- ½ tsp. Salt
- ½ tsp. nutmeg
- 1 tsp. cinnamon
- A tiny pinch of cloves
- ½ c. cold butter, cubed

Directions:

1. Set the oven to 375°F then grease an 8x8" baking dish with butter.
2. Mix the apple slices, cranberries, lemon juice, and sugar in a bowl. Pour the mixture into the baking dish.
3. In a separate bowl, make the topping by mixing the oats, flour, sugar, salt, nutmeg, cinnamon, and cloves. Blend in the butter using a pastry cutter.
4. Sprinkle the topping over the apples.
5. Bake for 30 minutes until the topping is brown and crisp.
6. Serve warm with ice cream or whipped cream.

Nutritional Information: Calories: 368, Fat: 12 g, Carbs: 66 g, Protein: 3 g, Sodium: 269 mg

116. Pineapple Casserole Dessert

Preparation Time: 15 minutes

Cooking Time: 65 minutes

Servings: 5

Ingredients:

- 1 c. butter
- 1 ½ c. white sugar
- 6 eggs
- 1 (15-oz.) can of crushed pineapple, drained
- 9 slices of bread, cubed
- ¼ c. sharp cheddar cheese, shredded

Directions:

1. Preheat the oven to 325°F.
2. Cream the butter and sugar together. Each at a time, beat in the eggs until fully incorporated. Fold in the pineapple and bread.
3. Into a 9x13" baking dish, pour the mixture.
4. Bake for 1 hour until the center springs back when touched lightly.
5. Sprinkle the cheese evenly over the top, and return to the oven to melt the cheese for 2–5 minutes.

Nutritional Information:

Calories: 284

Fat: 11 g

Carbs: 43 g

Protein: 4 g

Sodium: 243 mg

117. Lemon Poke Cake

Preparation Time: 15 minutes

Cooking Time: 30 minutes

Servings: 5

Ingredients:

- 1 boxed lemon cake, baked in a 9x13" pan and cooled
- 2 c. cooked lemon pudding, not yet set (reserve ¼ c. for drizzling)
- 1 (8 oz.) container of whipped dessert topping
- ½ c. white chocolate chips
- ½ c. chopped pecans

Directions:

1. To poke holes evenly throughout the baked cake (approximately 20–25 holes), use the handle of a wooden spoon.
2. Pour the lemon pudding over the cake, filling the holes. Use a rubber spatula to spread it evenly over the cake.
3. Spread the whipped topping over the top. Sprinkle on the white chips and pecans. Drizzle with remaining lemon pudding.
4. Let it chill for at least 4 hours. Overnight is best.

Nutritional Information:

Calories: 301

Carbs: 44 g

Fat: 12 g

Protein: 3 g

Sodium: 309 mg

118. Raspberry Cobbler

Preparation Time: 15 minutes

Cooking Time: 20 minutes

Servings: 5

Ingredients:

- 1 c. all-purpose flour
- 1 ½ c. white sugar, divided
- 1 tsp. Baking powder
- ½ tsp. salt
- 6 tbsps. cold butter
- ¼ c. boiling water
- 2 tbsps. cornstarch
- ¼ c. cold water
- 1 tbsp. lemon juice
- 4 c. fresh raspberries, rinsed and drained
- 1 tbsp. vanilla

Directions:

1. Heat the oven to 400°F. A baking sheet should be covered with aluminum foil.
2. In a large bowl, combine the flour, salt, baking soda, and half a cup of sugar. The mixture should have butter added until it resembles coarse crumbs.
3. Add ¼ cup of hot water to moisten the mixture evenly.
4. In another basin, combine the cornstarch with cold water to dissolve it. The remaining 1 cup of sugar, lemon juice, and raspberries should be added to the mixture.
5. Bring the ingredients to a boil while stirring continually in a cast iron skillet. Add the vanilla after pulling it off the heat.
6. Pour the batter into the skillet in spoonfuls.
7. Bake the skillet on a baking sheet lined with foil for 25 minutes or until the dough turns a golden brown color.

Nutritional Information:

Calories: 318

Fat: 9 g

Carbs: 58 g

Protein: 3 g

Sodium: 253 mg

119. Georgia Cobbler

Preparation Time: 15 minutes

Cooking Time: 20 minutes

Servings: 5

Ingredients:

- 16 c. fresh peaches, peeled and diced
- 3 c. sugar
- ⅓ c. all-purpose flour
- ½ tsp. cinnamon
- ¼ tsp. allspice
- 1 ½ tsps. vanilla
- ⅔ c. butter
- 2 packages of refrigerated pie dough
- ½ c. chopped pecans, toasted
- ¼ c. sugar
- Vanilla ice cream for serving

Directions:

1. Combine the peaches, sugar, flour, cinnamon, and allspice in a Dutch oven, and let it sit until the sugar dissolves.
2. Set it over medium-high heat and let it boil. Simmer for 10 minutes or until tender in low heat.
3. Remove it from the heat. Add the vanilla and butter, stirring until the butter melts. Preheat the oven to 475°F and coat a 9x13" baking dish with cooking spray.
4. Unfold two pie crusts. Sprinkle ¼ cup of pecans and 2 tablespoons of sugar evenly over 1 pie crust and top it with another. Roll it out to a 12-inch circle, gently pressing pecans into the pastry. Cut into 1 ½-inch strips.
5. Repeat with remaining pie crusts, pecans, and sugar. Spoon half of the peach mixture into the baking dish. Arrange half of the pastry strips in a lattice design over the peach mixture.
6. Bake for 20–25 minutes or until lightly browned. Spoon the remaining peach mixture over the baked pastry. Top with the remaining pastry strips in a lattice design. Bake for 15–18 more minutes.
7. Serve warm or cold with vanilla ice cream.

Nutritional Information: Calories: 374, Fat: 14 g, Carbs: 59 g, Protein: 4 g, Sodium: 182 mg

120. Praline Pumpkin Pudding

Preparation Time: 10 minutes

Cooking Time: 20 minutes

Servings: 5

Ingredients:

For the Bread Pudding:

- 4 large eggs
- 2 (15 oz.) cans of pumpkin purée
- 1 ½ c. milk
- ¾ c. half and half
- 1 c. white sugar
- 1 tsp. Ground cinnamon
- ½ tsp. Salt
- ½ tsp. ground nutmeg
- A pinch of ground cardamom
- 1 tsp. vanilla extract
- 1 loaf of French bread, cut into 1-inch pieces (about 10 c.)

For the Caramel-Pecan Sauce:

- 1 c. pecans, chopped
- 1 c. firmly packed light brown sugar
- ½ c. butter
- 3 tbsps. light corn syrup
- 1 tsp. vanilla extract

Directions:

1. Prepare the bread puddings: Whisk together the eggs, pumpkin, milk, half and half, sugar, cinnamon, salt, nutmeg, cardamom, and vanilla until well blended.
2. Add the bread pieces, stirring to coat thoroughly. Cover with plastic wrap, and chill for 8–24 hours.
3. Preheat the oven to 350°F. Spoon the bread mixture into 11 6-oz. lightly greased ramekins. (The ramekins will be full, and the mixture will mound slightly.)
4. Bake for 50 minutes, shielding with foil after 30 minutes.
5. During the last 15 minutes of baking, prepare the caramel-pecan sauce. Heat the pecans in a medium skillet over medium-low heat, stirring, for 3–5 minutes or until lightly toasted and fragrant.
6. Cook the brown sugar, butter, and corn syrup in a small saucepan over medium heat, occasionally stirring for 3–4 minutes or until the sugar is dissolved. Take it away from the heat and stir in the vanilla and pecans.

7. Remove the bread puddings from the oven and drizzle with caramel-pecan sauce. Bake for 5 minutes or until the sauce is thoroughly heated and begins to bubble.

Nutritional Information:

Calories: 356

Fat: 24 g

Carbs: 29 g

Protein: 5 g

Sodium: 162 mg

121. Tipsy Baked Winter Fruit

Preparation Time: 15 minutes

Cooking Time: 50 minutes

Servings: 5

Ingredients:

- 10 oz. dried figs, trimmed and halved
- 7 oz. dried apricots
- 5 oz. dried apples
- 2 c. apple cider
- ⅔ c. dry sherry
- ½ c. golden raisins
- 2 navel oranges, peeled and sectioned
- 1 (3-inch) cinnamon stick Brown
- Optional: Whipped cream for serving

Directions:

1. Place all the ingredients EXCEPT the orange slices for garnishing in a 7x11" baking dish, and gently toss to combine. Cover with aluminum foil, and chill for 12–24 hours.
2. Preheat the oven to 350°F. Bake the fruit mixture, covered, for 45–50 minutes or until it is thoroughly heated and the fruit is soft.
3. Let it stand, covered, for 15 minutes. Remove and discard the cinnamon stick. Serve with whipped cream, if desired.

Nutritional Information:

Calories: 496

Fat: 8 g

Carbs: 104 g

Protein: 2 g

Sodium: 90 mg

122. Chocolate Pecan Pie

Preparation Time: 15 minutes

Cooking Time: 20 minutes

Servings: 5

Ingredients:

- Unbaked 9" pie crust
- ⅔ c. evaporated milk
- 2 tbsps. unsalted butter
- 1 c. semisweet chocolate chips
- 2 eggs, beaten
- 1 c. granulated sugar
- 2 tbsps. All-purpose flour
- ¼ tsp. salt
- 1 tsp. vanilla extract
- 1 c. chopped pecans

Directions:

1. If you haven't already done so, place the pie dough in a 9" pan. Set the oven to 375°F.
2. Add the evaporated milk, butter, and chocolate chips to a saucepan set over low heat. Cook the chocolate while constantly stirring until it melts.
3. As soon as the butter and chocolate have melted, remove the pan from the heat. Keep the milk from boiling.
4. Chocolate should be added to a mixing bowl. Eggs, brown sugar, all-purpose flour, salt, vanilla extract, and pecans should all be added to the bowl.
5. Blend thoroughly by whisking. Fill the pie crust with the filling. For 35 minutes or until the middle is firm, bake the pie.
6. When the pie is done, a knife should come out clean, slightly off the center. Before serving, let the pie cool for at least 30 minutes after removing it from the oven.

Nutritional Information: Calories: 137, Total Fat: 6.5 g, Saturated Fat: 0.9 g, Cholesterol: 0 mg , Total Carbs: 16.9 g , Sugar: 0 g , Fiber: 2.6 g , Sodium: 203 mg , Potassium: 158 mg , Protein: 4 g

123. Lemon Pecan Pie

Preparation Time: 15 minutes

Cooking Time: 20 minutes

Servings: 5

Ingredients:

- Unbaked 9" deep dish pie crust
- 4 eggs, beaten
- 6 tbsps. unsalted butter softened
- 1 c. light corn syrup
- ½ c. light brown sugar
- 2 tsps. grated lemon zest
- ¼ c. lemon juice
- 3 tbsps. all-purpose flour
- 1 ¼ c. chopped pecans

Directions:

1. If you haven't previously, place the pie dough in a 9" deep dish pie pan. Set the oven to 450°F. With a fork, prick the pie crust all over. The pie crust should not expand while baking.
2. The pie crust should be faintly browned after 7 minutes in the oven. Before filling, remove from the oven and allow cool fully.
3. Set the oven to 350°F. In a mixing bowl, combine the eggs, butter, corn syrup, brown sugar, lemon juice, lemon zest, and all-purpose flour.
4. The filling should be blended and smooth after whisking. Into the pie crust, pour the filling after stirring in the pecans.
5. Bake the pie for 40 minutes or until the middle is firm. When the pie is done, a knife put into the center should come out without batter.
6. During the final 25 minutes of baking, with aluminum foil, shield the pie crust's edges to keep them from burning. Before serving, remove from the oven and let cool fully.

Nutritional Information:

Calories: 163

Fat: 14 g

Carbohydrates: 3 g

Protein: 8 g

124. Coconut Pecan Pie

Preparation Time: 15 minutes

Cooking Time: 20 minutes

Servings: 5

Ingredients:

- Unbaked 9" pie crust
- 3 eggs
- ¾ c. granulated sugar
- ¾ c. dark corn syrup
- 1 tsp. vanilla extract
- ⅛ tsp. salt
- ¼ c. unsalted butter, melted
- 1 tbsp. unsweetened cocoa powder
- 2 c. pecan halves
- ½ c. sweetened flaked coconut

Directions:

1. Place the pie crust in a 9" pie pan if you have not already done this step. Preheat the oven to 350°F.
2. Add the eggs, granulated sugar, dark corn syrup, vanilla extract, salt, butter, and cocoa powder in a mixing bowl. Using a mixer on medium speed, beat until well blended and the filling is smooth.
3. Turn the mixer off and stir in the pecans and coconut. Pour the filling into the pie crust.
4. Bake for 50 minutes or until the filling is set. A knife inserted off the center of the pie should come out clean when ready. Remove from the oven and cool completely before serving.

Nutritional Information:

Calories: 163

Fat: 14 g

Carbohydrates: 3 g

Protein: 8 g

125. Custard Pecan Pie

Preparation Time: 15 minutes

Cooking Time: 20 minutes

Servings: 5

Ingredients:

- 3 eggs, separated and at room temperature
- ⅛ tsp. salt
- 1 ¼ c. + 2 tbsps. granulated sugar
- ½ tsp. vanilla extract
- 1 c. whole milk
- 2 tbsps. cornstarch
- 1 c. chopped pecans, toasted
- ¼ c. unsalted butter
- Baked 9" pie crust, cooled

Directions:

1. In a mixing bowl, add the egg whites and salt. Using a mixer on medium speed, beat until the egg whites are foamy.
2. Add ¼ cup + 2 tablespoons of granulated sugar, 1 tablespoon at a time, to the egg whites. Add the vanilla extract and beat the egg whites until stiff peaks form.
3. In a small bowl, add the egg yolks and milk. Whisk until combined. Over medium heat, add the egg yolk mixture, 1 cup of granulated sugar, and cornstarch in a saucepan. Stir constantly and bring the filling to a boil. Boil the filling for 1 minute.
4. Take away the pan from the heat and add the pecans and butter to the pan. Stir until the butter melts and all the ingredients are well combined.
5. Spoon the filling into the pie crust. Spread the egg white meringue over the filling. Make sure the meringue is spread to the pie crust. This will keep the meringue from shrinking.
6. Preheat the oven to 400°F. Bake for 8-10 minutes or until the meringue is lightly browned. Remove from the oven and cool completely before serving.

Nutritional Information: Calories: 72, Total Fat: 0.3 g, Saturated Fat: 0.1 g, Cholesterol: 0 mg, Total Carbs: 16.3 g, Sugar: 4.9 g, Fiber: 3 g, Sodium: 28 mg, Potassium: 369 mg, Protein: 1.6 g

126. Coffee Pecan Pie

Preparation Time: 15 minutes

Cooking Time: 20 minutes

Servings: 5

Ingredients:

- 1 egg, separated and at room temperature
- ¼ tsp. salt
- ¼ c. granulated sugar
- 1 tbsp. instant coffee granules
- ¼ c. boiling water
- 2 ¼ c. miniature marshmallows
- ½ tsp. almond extract
- 1 ½ c. finely chopped pecans
- 2 c. whipping cream
- Grated chocolate for garnish, optional

Directions:

1. In a mixing bowl, add the egg white and salt. Using a mixer on medium speed, beat until stiff peaks form.
2. Add the granulated sugar and beat until the sugar is well combined and the egg whites are moist but very stiff. Spray an 8" pie pan with nonstick cooking spray. Spread the beaten egg white into the pie pan to form a crust.
3. Preheat the oven to 400°F. Bake for 10 minutes. The crust should be lightly browned and firm. Remove the crust from the oven. Cool the pie crust entirely before using.
4. Coffee granules and boiling water should be combined in a saucepan over medium heat. Stir the coffee until it melts. Marshmallows should be added and stirred until melted. Egg yolk should be added to a small bowl. Blend until well combined.
5. To the egg yolk, add 2 teaspoons of the marshmallow mixture. Add the egg yolk to the pan after whisking everything together. Cook for 1 minute while stirring continuously. When the filling starts to set, remove the pan from the heat and continue stirring.
6. Add the pecans and almond extract after that. In a mixing bowl, add 1 cup of whipping cream. Using a mixer on medium speed, beat until soft peaks form.
7. Fold the whipping cream into the marshmallow filling. Spread the filling over the crust. Refrigerate until well chilled
8. When ready to serve, add the remaining cup of whipping cream to a mixing bowl. Using a mixer on medium speed, beat until soft peaks form.
9. Spread the whipped cream over the top of the pie. Sprinkle the grated chocolate over the top if desired.

Nutritional Information:

Calories: 72

Total Fat: 0.3 g

Saturated Fat: 0.1 g

Cholesterol: 0 mg

Total Carbs: 16.3 g

Sugar: 4.9 g

Fiber: 3 g

Sodium: 28 mg

Potassium: 369 mg

Protein: 1.6 g

127. Lemon Lime Chess Pie

Preparation Time: 15 minutes

Cooking Time: 20 minutes

Servings: 5

Ingredients:

- Unbaked 9" pie crust
- 1 ½ c. granulated sugar
- 1 tbsp. All-purpose flour
- ¼ tsp. salt
- 1 tbsp. plain yellow cornmeal
- ¼ c. unsalted butter, melted
- ¼ c. whole milk
- 1 tsp. grated lemon zest
- 1 tsp. grated lime zest
- ⅓ c. fresh lime juice
- 1 tbsp. fresh lemon juice
- 4 eggs, beaten

Directions:

1. If you haven't already done so, place the pie dough in a 9" pan. Set the oven to 450°F.
2. With a fork, prick the pie crust all over. For 8 minutes, bake. Before filling, take the pie crust out of the oven and let it cool.
3. Granulated sugar, all-purpose flour, salt, cornmeal, butter, milk, lemon zest, lemon zest, lemon juice, and eggs should all be combined in a mixing bowl.
4. When the filling is thoroughly incorporated, beat it with a mixer on medium speed. Fill the pie crust with the filling.
5. Set the oven to 350°F. Bake the pie for 40 minutes or until the middle is firm. Use aluminum foil to protect the pie crust's edges from burning.
6. When ready, the center will still wiggle a little. As it sets, the pie will continue to solidify. Before serving, remove from the oven and let cool fully.

Nutritional Information: Calories: 298 , Total Fat: 6.5 g , Saturated Fat: 1.3 g, Cholesterol: 0 mg, Sodium: 139 mg, Total Carbs: 48.2 g, Fiber: 7.6 g, Sugar: 12.1 g, Protein: 16 g

128. Brown Sugar Chess Pie

Preparation Time: 15 minutes

Cooking Time: 20 minutes

Servings: 5

Ingredients:

- Unbaked 8" pie crust
- ½ c. granulated sugar
- ½ c. light brown sugar
- 1 tbsp. all-purpose flour
- 1 tbsp. plain white cornmeal
- A pinch of salt
- 3 eggs
- 1 tsp. White vinegar
- ½ tsp. vanilla extract
- ¼ c. whole milk
- ¼ c. unsalted butter, melted

Directions:

1. Place the pie crust in an 8" pie pan if you have not already done this step. In a mixing bowl, add the granulated sugar, brown sugar, all-purpose flour, cornmeal, and salt.
2. Stir until well combined. Add the eggs, white vinegar, vanilla extract, milk, and butter to the bowl. Using a mixer on medium speed, beat for 2 minutes.
3. The filling should be thoroughly combined and smooth. Pour the filling into the pie crust.
4. Set the oven to 350°F. For 30 minutes or until the middle is nearly set, bake the pie. When ready, the center will still wiggle a little.
5. As it sets, the pie will continue to solidify. Before serving, remove from the oven and let cool fully.

Nutritional Information: Calories: 298, Total Fat: 6.5 g, Saturated Fat: 1.3 g, Cholesterol: 0 mg, Sodium: 139 mg, Total Carbs: 48.2 g, Fiber: 7.6 g, Sugar: 12.1 g, Protein: 16 g

129. Orange Chess Pie

Preparation Time: 15 minutes

Cooking Time: 20 minutes

Servings: 5

Ingredients:

- Unbaked 9" pie crust
- ½ c. unsalted butter softened
- 1 c. granulated sugar
- 3 eggs, beaten
- 3 tbsps. plain white cornmeal
- 1 tbsp. + 1 tsp. grated orange zest
- ½ c. orange juice

Directions:

1. If you haven't already done so, place the pie dough in a 9" pan. Set the oven to 350°F. Add the butter and white sugar to a mixing bowl.
2. Beat ingredients with a mixer on medium speed until smooth and thoroughly combined. Add the eggs and mix everything until it's smooth.
3. Add cornmeal, orange juice, and zest to the bowl. Mix thoroughly until the filling is smooth.
4. Fill the pie crust with the filling. A knife inserted in the center of the pie should come out clean after 45 minutes of baking.
5. When ready, the center will still wiggle a little. Its pie will continue to firm up as it sets. Remove from the oven and cool completely before serving.

Nutritional Information:

Calories: 237

Total Fat: 9 g

Saturated Fat: 1 g

Cholesterol: 0 mg

Sodium: 520 mg

Total Carbs: 2293.3 g

Fiber: 5.9 g

Sugar: 3.7 g

Protein: 11.1 g

130. Tangerine Chess Pie

Preparation Time: 15 minutes

Cooking Time: 20 minutes

Servings: 5

Ingredients:

- Unbaked 9" pie crust
- 1 ½ c. granulated sugar
- 1 tbsp. All-purpose flour
- ¼ tsp. salt
- 1 tbsp. plain yellow cornmeal
- ¼ c. unsalted butter, melted
- ¼ c. whole milk
- 2 tsps. grated tangerine zest
- ⅓ c. fresh tangerine juice
- 1 tbsp. lemon juice
- 4 eggs, beaten

Directions:

1. If you haven't already done so, place the pie dough in a 9" pan. Set the oven to 450°F. With a fork, prick the pie crust all over.
2. For 8 minutes, bake. Before filling, take the pie crust out of the oven and let it cool.
3. Granulated sugar, all-purpose flour, salt, cornmeal, butter, milk, tangerine zest, juice, lemon juice, and eggs should all be combined in a mixing dish.
4. When the filling is thoroughly incorporated, beat it with a mixer on medium speed. Fill the pie crust with the filling.
5. Set the oven to 350°F. Bake the pie for 40 minutes or until the middle is firm. Use aluminum foil to protect the pie crust's edges from burning.
6. When ready, the center will still wiggle a little. As it sets, the pie will continue to solidify. Before serving, remove from the oven and let cool fully.

Nutritional Information: Calories: 213, Total Fat: 11.8 g, Saturated Fat: 2.2 g, Cholesterol: 0 mg, Total Carbs: 14.7 g, Sugar: 8 g, Fiber: 4.5 g, Sodium: 31 mg, Potassium: 872 mg, Protein: 17.3 g

131. Coconut Macadamia Chess Pie

Preparation Time: 15 minutes

Cooking Time: 20 minutes

Servings: 5

Ingredients:

- Unbaked 9" pie crust
- 1 c. granulated sugar
- 3 eggs
- 1 c. light corn syrup
- ¼ c. whipping cream
- 1 tbsp. unsalted butter, melted
- 1 tsp. vanilla extract
- ¾ c. macadamia nuts, chopped
- 1 c. sweetened flaked coconut
- Whipped cream, optional

Directions:

1. If you haven't already done so, place the pie dough in a 9" pan. The pie crust should be frozen for 15 minutes.
2. Set the oven to 425°F. Bake the pie crust for 8 minutes after removing it from the freezer. Golden brown should describe the pie crust. Before filling, take the crust out of the oven and let it cool.
3. Granulated sugar, eggs, corn syrup, whipping cream, butter, and vanilla extract should all be combined in a mixing dish.
4. Blend and smooth out the filling with a whisk. Add the coconut and macadamia nuts after mixing. The filling should be poured into a pie shell.
5. Set the oven to 350°F. A knife placed in the center of the pie should come clean after 55 minutes of baking. If necessary, wrap the pie crust's edges with aluminum foil to keep them from burning.
6. Before serving, remove from the oven and let cool thoroughly. If desired, top slices with whipped cream when serving.

Nutritional Information: Calories: 213, Total Fat: 11.8 g, Saturated Fat: 2.2 g, Cholesterol: 0 mg, Total Carbs: 14.7 g, Sugar: 8 g, Fiber: 4.5 g, Sodium: 31 mg, Potassium: 872 mg, Protein: 17.3 g

132. Coconut Banana Cream Pie

Preparation Time: 10 minutes

Cooking Time: 43 minutes

Servings: 5

Ingredients:

- ¾ c. granulated sugar
- ¼ c. cornstarch
- ½ tsp. salt
- 2 c. whole milk
- 3 eggs, separated and at room temperature
- 1 c. toasted coconut
- 1 ¼ tsp. vanilla extract
- 2 bananas, sliced
- Baked 9" pie crust, cooled
- ¼ tsp. Cream of tartar
- ⅛ tsp. salt
- ⅓ c. granulated sugar

Directions:

1. In a saucepan over medium heat, add ¾ cup of granulated sugar, cornstarch, salt, milk, and egg yolks.
2. Stir constantly and cook for about 8 minutes or until the filling thickens and bubbles. Take away the pan from the heat and stir in the coconut and vanilla extract.
3. Place the bananas in the pie crust. Spoon the coconut filling over the bananas. Add the egg whites, cream of tartar, and salt in a mixing bowl.
4. Using a mixer on medium speed, beat until the egg whites are foamy. Add ⅓ cup of granulated sugar, 1 tablespoon at a time, and beat the egg whites until stiff peaks form.
5. The meringue must be spread over the filling as well as the crust.
6. Preheat the oven to 325°F. Bake for 20 minutes or until the meringue is golden brown.
7. Remove from the oven and cool the pie entirely at room temperature. You can serve the pie once cooled, but the pie tastes best if chilled at least 4 hours before serving.

Nutritional Information:

Calories: 435

Fat: 30 g

Carbohydrates: 34 g

Protein: 16 g

133. German Chocolate Chess Pies

Preparation Time: 10 minutes

Cooking Time: 30 minutes

Servings: 5

Ingredients:

- 2 unbaked pie crusts, 8" size
- 4 oz. sweet baking chocolate
- ¼ c. unsalted butter
- 13 oz. can evaporate milk
- 1 ½ c. granulated sugar
- 3 tbsps. Cornstarch
- ⅛ tsp. salt
- 2 eggs
- 1 tsp. vanilla extract
- 1 ⅓ c. sweetened flaked coconut
- ½ c. chopped pecans

Directions:

1. In two 8" pie pans, if you haven't previously, place the pie crust. The chocolate and butter should be placed in a saucepan over low heat.
2. Cook the chocolate and butter, stirring regularly, until the butter melts and the mixture is smooth. Add the evaporated milk after taking the pan off the heat. Stir thoroughly to mix.
3. Add the eggs, vanilla extract, cornstarch, salt, and granulated sugar to the pan. The filling should be blended and smooth after whisking.
4. Fill the pie crust with the filling. Over the filling, scatter the coconut and pecans.
5. Set the oven to 375°F. Bake the pies for 45 minutes or until the centers are nearly set. When ready, the center will still wiggle a little.
6. Pies will continue to solidify as they cool. Before serving, remove from the oven and let cool fully.

Nutritional Information: Calories: 143, Total Fat: 8.4 g, Saturated Fat: 2.2 g, Cholesterol: 218 mg, Total Carbs: 9.3 g, Sugar: 4.2 g, Fiber: 1.1 g, Sodium: 98 mg, Potassium: 408 mg, Protein: 8.9 g

134. Lemon Meringue Pie

Preparation Time: 15 minutes

Cooking Time: 20 minutes

Servings: 6

Ingredients:

- 2 c. + 2 tbsps. granulated sugar
- ⅓ c. cornstarch
- ¼ tsp. salt
- 1 ½ c. cold water
- ½ c. lemon juice
- 5 eggs, separated and at room temperature
- 2 tbsps. unsalted butter
- 3 tsps. grated lemon zest
- Baked 9" pie crust, cooled
- ¼ tsp. Cream of tartar
- ½ tsp. vanilla extract

Directions:

1. Add 1 ½ cups of granulated sugar, cornstarch, salt, cold water, and lemon juice in a saucepan. Whisk until well combined. In a mixing bowl, add the egg yolks.
2. Using a mixer on medium speed, beat for 2 minutes or until the egg yolks are thickened and lemon colored. Add the mixture from the saucepan and mix until well combined. Add the entire filling back to the pan. Add the butter and lemon zest to the pan.
3. Stir the filling constantly while cooking. Place the saucepan over medium heat. Cook for about 8-9 minutes or until the filling thickens and bubbles.
4. Cook the filling for 1 additional minute after the filling boils. Remove the pan from the heat and spoon the filling into the pie crust.
5. Add the egg whites, cream of tartar, and vanilla extract in a mixing bowl. Using a mixer on medium speed, beat the egg whites until foamy.
6. Add ½ cup and 2 tablespoons of granulated sugar, adding only a tablespoon at a time, to the egg whites. The sugar should be well combined before adding the next tablespoon. Beat until stiff peaks form.
7. The meringue must be spread over the top of the pie. Be sure to spread the meringue to the crust. This will keep the meringue from weeping.
8. Preheat the oven to 350°F. Bake for 12-15 minutes or until the meringue is golden brown. Remove from the oven and cool completely at room temperature before serving.
9. Refrigerate the pie before serving if desired. The flavor of the pie will improve upon chilling. Store the pie in the refrigerator.

Nutritional Information:

Calories: 143

Total Fat: 8.4 g

Saturated Fat: 2.2 g

Cholesterol: 218 mg

Total Carbs: 9.3 g

Sugar: 4.2 g

Fiber: 1.1 g

Sodium: 98 mg

Potassium: 408 mg

Protein: 8.9 g

135. Old Fashioned Whipped Lemon Cream Pie

Preparation Time: 15 minutes

Cooking Time: 20 minutes

Servings: 5

Ingredients:

- ⅔ c. water
- ⅓ c. + 2 tbsps. fresh lemon juice
- 4-serving size box of lemon jello
- ½ c. granulated sugar
- 1 tsp. grated lemon zest
- 1 c. evaporated milk
- 9" graham cracker pie crust

Directions:

1. Add the water and ⅓ cup lemon juice to a saucepan over medium heat. Bring the liquids to a boil and remove the pan from the heat. Stir in the lemon jello and granulated sugar.
2. Stir until the jello and sugar are dissolved. Stir in the lemon zest. Refrigerate the filling until it is the consistency of an egg white. Add the evaporated milk to a mixing bowl. Freeze the milk until ice crystals form around the edges. This takes about 15 minutes in my freezer.
3. Remove the bowl from the freezer. Using a mixer on medium speed, beat until stiff peaks form. This takes about 1 minute with my mixer.
4. Add 2 tablespoons of lemon juice and beat for about 2 minutes or until stiff peaks form. Freeze the milk for an extra few minutes if needed to make sure the milk is very cold. The milk will not whip if it does not have ice crystals around the edges.
5. Turn the mixer off. Gently fold the chilled lemon filling into the whipped milk. Spread the filling in the graham cracker crust.
6. Refrigerate for 4 hours or until the pie is firm before serving.

Nutritional Information: Calories: 321, Protein: 11 g, Carbohydrates: 25 g, Fat: 7 g

Cholesterol: 123 mg

Sodium: 50 mg

Potassium: 139 mg

Phosphorus: 130 mg

Calcium: 30 mg

Fiber: 2

136. Orange Meringue Pie

Preparation Time: 15 minutes

Cooking Time: 20 minutes

Servings: 5

Ingredients:

- 2 c. granulated sugar
- ¼ c. + 2 tbsps. Cornstarch
- ¼ tsp. salt
- 1 ½ tsps. grated orange zest
- 3 c. orange juice
- 4 eggs, separated and at room temperature
- ¼ c. + 2 tbsps. lemon juice
- 3 tbsps. unsalted butter
- Baked 9" pie crust, cooled
- ¼ tsp. cream of tartar
- Orange slices for garnish, optional

Directions:

1. Over medium heat, add 1 ½ cups of granulated sugar, cornstarch, salt, orange zest, orange juice, egg yolks, and lemon juice in a saucepan.
2. Stir constantly and bring to a boil. Add the butter to the pan. Stir until the butter melts and the filling thickens and bubbles.
3. Remove the pan from the heat and spoon the filling into the pie crust.
4. In a mixing bowl, add the egg whites and cream of tartar. Using a mixer on medium speed, beat until the egg whites are foamy.
5. Slowly add ½ cup of granulated sugar to the egg whites. Beat until stiff peaks form. Spread the meringue over the pie making sure to spread the meringue to the crust.
6. Preheat the oven to 350°F. Bake for 10-12 minutes or until the meringue is lightly browned.
7. Remove from the oven and cool the pie entirely at room temperature. Refrigerate the pie for 8 hours before serving. Garnish with orange slices if desired.

Nutritional Information:

Calories: 435

Fat: 30 g

Carbohydrates: 34 g

Protein: 16 g

137. Vanilla Cream Pie

Preparation Time: 15 minutes

Cooking Time: 20 minutes

Servings: 5

Ingredients:

- 1 ¼ c. granulated sugar
- ⅓ c. cornstarch
- ¼ tsp. salt
- 4 egg yolks, beaten
- 4 c. whole milk
- 2 tbsps. unsalted butter
- 1 ½ tsps. vanilla extract
- 4 egg whites, at room temperature
- ¼ tsp. cream of tartar
- Baked 9" pie crust

Directions:

1. Add milk, cornstarch, salt, egg yolks, and 1 cup of granulated sugar to a saucepan set over medium heat until blended and smooth.
2. Cook the filling, frequently stirring, until it thickens and bubbles. On my stove, this takes about 8 minutes. Butter and vanilla essence are added after the pan has been taken off the heat. While you make the meringue, cover the pan and let the filling cool.
3. Add both the egg whites and cream of tartar to a mixing bowl. Beat the egg whites with a mixer on medium speed until frothy.
4. To the egg whites, gradually incorporate ¼ cup of granulated sugar. Until stiff peaks appear, beat.
5. The filling should be poured into a pie shell. The meringue should be applied to the entire pie, including the crust. Set the oven to 350°F. Bake the meringue for 12 minutes or until golden brown.
6. Before serving, remove from the oven and allow to cool fully at room temperature. It is recommended to serve the pie cold.

Nutritional Information:

Calories: 435

Fat: 30 g

Carbohydrates: 34 g

Protein: 16 g

138. White Chocolate Banana Cream Pie

Preparation Time: 15 minutes

Cooking Time: 20 minutes

Servings: 5

Ingredients:

- 4 oz. white chocolate bar, finely chopped
- 1 c. whole milk
- 1 ½ tsps. vanilla extract
- 3 tbsps. granulated sugar
- 2 tbsps. cornstarch
- 3 egg yolks
- 1 tbsp. unsalted butter
- 1 c. + 2 tbsps. whipping cream
- 2 tbsps. chocolate syrup
- 2 bananas, sliced
- 3 tbsps. lemon juice
- Baked 9" pie crust, cooled

Directions:

1. Place 2 ounces of white chocolate in a double boiler. Stir until the white chocolate melts. Remove the pan from the heat.
2. Line a baking sheet with aluminum foil. Spread the white chocolate on the aluminum foil. Cool until the white chocolate feels tacky.
3. Using a vegetable peeler, pull the peeler across the white chocolate until you have curls. Place the white chocolate curls in the refrigerator.
4. Over medium heat, add the milk, vanilla extract, granulated sugar, cornstarch, and egg yolks in a saucepan. Stir constantly and cook until the filling thickens and bubbles.
5. Take away the pan from the heat and add the butter and remaining white chocolate. Stir until the butter and white chocolate melt.
6. In a mixing bowl, add the whipping cream. Using a mixer on medium speed, beat until soft peaks form. Turn off the mixer and gently fold the whipped cream and chocolate syrup into the filling.
7. In a small bowl, add the bananas and lemon juice. Toss until the bananas are coated in the lemon juice.
8. Place the bananas in the pie crust. Spoon the filling over the bananas. Put the pie in the fridge for at least 4 hours before serving.

Nutritional Information:

Calories: 321

Protein: 11 g

Carbohydrates: 25 g

Fat: 7 g

Cholesterol: 123 mg

Sodium: 50 mg

Potassium: 139 mg

Phosphorus: 130 mg

Calcium: 30 mg

139. Tropical Pie

Preparation Time: 10 minutes

Cooking Time: 20 minutes

Servings: 5

Ingredients:

- 8 oz. can of crushed pineapple with juice
- 1 tbsp. granulated sugar
- 1 c. whole milk
- 4-serving size package of vanilla cook-and-serve pudding mix
- 1 c. sour cream
- 1 ½ c. sweetened flaked coconut
- 1 banana, peeled and sliced
- Baked 9" pie crust, cooled
- 1 ½ c. Cool Whip, thawed

Directions:

1. Over medium heat, add the pineapple with juice, granulated sugar, milk, and dry vanilla pudding in a saucepan. Stir constantly and cook until the filling comes to a boil.
2. Remove the pan from the heat. Put the sour cream in a small bowl. Add 2 teaspoons of hot filling to the sour cream.
3. Whisk until well combined, and add the sour cream to the pan. Stir until combined, and add 1 cup of coconut to the pan. Stir until well combined.
4. Refrigerate the filling until well chilled. Place the banana slices in the bottom of the pie crust. Spoon the filling over the banana. The pie's top should be covered with Cool Whip. Sprinkle ½ cup of coconut over the top of the pie. Refrigerate for 2 hours before serving.

Nutritional Information:

Calories: 120

Fat: 7 g

Carbs: 10 g

Protein: 2 g

Fiber: 6 g

140. Grape Juice Pie

Preparation Time: 15 minutes

Cooking Time: 20 minutes

Servings: 5

Ingredients:

- ¾ c. + 1 tbsp. granulated sugar
- ¼ c. cornstarch
- 1 ½ c. grape juice
- 1 egg, beaten
- 2 tbsps. unsalted butter
- 2 tbsps. lemon juice
- Baked 9" pie crust
- 1 c. whipping cream

Directions:

1. In a saucepan over low heat, add ¾ cups of granulated sugar, cornstarch, and grape juice. Stir constantly and cook until the filling thickens and bubbles.
2. Cook for 1 additional minute after the filling boils. Remove the pan from the heat.
3. Add the beaten egg to a small bowl. Add 2 teaspoons of hot filling to the egg. Whisk quickly so the egg does not cook. Whisk until combined, and add the egg to the saucepan.
4. Add the butter and lemon juice to the pan. Stir until well combined and place the pan back over the heat. Bring the filling back to a boil and cook for 1 minute.
5. Remove the pan from the heat. Cool the filling at room temperature.
6. Spoon the filling into the pie crust. Refrigerate the pie until well chilled or at least 4 hours. Add the whipping cream and 1 tablespoon granulated sugar to a mixing bowl.
7. Using a mixer on medium speed, beat until stiff peaks form. Spread the whipped cream over the pie and refrigerate until chilled before serving.

Nutritional Information:

Calories: 160

Fat: 2.6 g

Carbs: 31 g

Protein: 6 g

Fiber: 6

CONCLUSION

Thank you for making it to the end!

These homemade recipes enable us to modify fast food items and create a dinner that is well-assembled and requires less effort to make than a regular meal. Although processing might reduce a product's nutritional value, replacing lost nutrients with fresh, nutrient-dense ingredients can help compensate for it.

The word "casserole," according to food historians, is derived from the Classical Greek word "kuathos," which meant "cup" and, over time, evolved into the Old French word "cause" before becoming the word "casserole." Eventually, the name came to refer to the baking vessel and the cooking method where food is slowly baked in a low oven. The nicest aspect is that we can combine readily available items from our kitchen with seasonal, fresh food.

You'll have more time to spend with your loved ones if you try the really easy and tasty recipes in this cookbook. While dinner bubbles and browns in the oven, imagine having time to read a nice book, catch up on household tasks, or relax after a long day at work. When you include healthful slow-cooked dishes, like casseroles, in your diet, it's simple to achieve that goal. This book has walked you step-by-step through the process of preparing nutritious one-dish meals and how to modify any classic casserole recipe to make it healthier.

Enjoy your recipes!

INDEX

Printed in Great Britain
by Amazon

32720231R00101